CAMBRIDGE
UNIVERSITY PRESS

Cambridge
Global English

WORKBOOK 11

Ingrid Wisniewska

CAMBRIDGE
UNIVERSITY PRESS

Shaftesbury Road, Cambridge CB2 8EA, United Kingdom

One Liberty Plaza, 20th Floor, New York, NY 10006, USA

477 Williamstown Road, Port Melbourne, VIC 3207, Australia

314–321, 3rd Floor, Plot 3, Splendor Forum, Jasola District Centre, New Delhi – 110025, India

103 Penang Road, #05–06/07, Visioncrest Commercial, Singapore 238467

Cambridge University Press is part of the University of Cambridge.

It furthers the University's mission by disseminating knowledge in the pursuit of education, learning and research at the highest international levels of excellence.

www.cambridge.org
Information on this title: www.cambridge.org/9781009398831

© Cambridge University Press & Assessment 2024

First published 2024

20 19 18 17 16 15 14 13 12 11 10 9 8 7 6 5 4 3 2 1

Printed in Malaysia by Vivar Printing

A catalogue record for this publication is available from the British Library

ISBN 978-1-009-39883-1 Workbook with Digital Access (2 Years)

Additional resources for this publication at www.cambridge.org/go

〉Acknowledgements

The authors and publishers acknowledge the following sources of copyright material and are grateful for the permissions granted. While every effort has been made, it has not always been possible to identify the sources of all the material used, or to trace all copyright holders. If any omissions are brought to our notice, we will be happy to include the appropriate acknowledgements on reprinting.

Unit 4: Chart showing participation by gender and broad activity types from 'Sport participation in England' by Lukas Audickas, 14 December 2017, House of Commons Library, Open Parliament Licence v3.0; chart showing levels of activity from article 'One million more active in England', 17th October 2019, used with the permission of Sports England; table created from 'How has access to primary education changed?' data source UNESCO for the year 2019, CC-BY by the author Max Roser from OurWorldinData.org.

Thanks to the following for permission to reproduce images:

Cover image Artur Debat/GI; *Inside* **Unit 1** Prostock-Studio/GI; Martinedoucet/GI; Average Teen Circadian Cycle diagram from NIGMS; Kali9/GI; Freder/GI; Xavier Lorenzo/GI; Gawrav/GI; Pixologicstudio/Science Photo Library/GI; **Unit 2** William Reagan/GI; Maridav/GI; Go Ga/GI; Cavan Images/GI; Andrea Comi/GI; Justin Paget/GI; Markus Daniel/GI; Fatcamera/GI; **Unit 3** Fcafotodigital/GI; Cherriesjd/GI; Kajakiki/GI; Photomaru/GI; Somyot Techapuwapat/GI; Imgorthand/GI; Benoist Sebire/GI; Mint Images/GI; Manuwe/GI; Tunart/GI; **Unit 4** Medianews Group/Reading Eagle/GI; Martin Novak/GI; SDI Productions/GI; Tasos Katopodis/GI; Ezra Shaw/GI; Lightfieldstudios/GI; Aleksandarnakic/GI; Jordan Siemens/GI; Martin Novak/GI; **Unit 5** Tara Moore/GI; Morsa Images/GI; Yagi Studio/GI; Solstock/GI; Franckreporter/GI; Pakin Songmor/GI; Peeterv/GI; Nurphoto/GI; Thomas Barwick/GI; Daisy-Daisy/GI; Orbon Alija/GI; PeopleImages/GI; Mixmedia/GI; **Unit 6** Patrick Landmann/Science Photo Library/GI; Scibak/GI; Andriy Onufriyenko/GI; Adventtr/GI; Encyclopaedia Britannica/GI; Majority World/GI; Klaus Vedfelt/GI; Peter Cade/GI; Peter Dazeley/GI; Peter Cade/GI; .Shock/GI; Salihkilic/GI; **Unit 7** Marko Geber/GI; Andreypopov/GI; Print Collector/GI; Hispanolistic/GI; Robert Daly/GI; Hadynyah/GI; Huephotography/GI; **Unit 8** Svetlana Lavereva/GI; Mayur Kakade/GI; Tetra Images/GI; Solstock/GI; Marc Dufresne/GI; Mayur Kakade/GI; Francesco Riccardo Iacomino/GI; Ilbusca/GI; Dianahirsch/GI; Hill Street Studios/GI; Gremlin/GI; **Unit 9** Kelvin Murray/GI; Coldsnowstorm/GI; Elenabs/GI; Westend61/GI; SDI Productions/GI; Morsa Images/GI; Cokada/GI; Motortion/GI; Pixelfit/GI; **Unit 10** Catherine Falls Commercial/GI; Jacoblund/GI; Hinterhaus Productions/GI; Richard Drury/GI; Drazen/GI; Kali9/GI; Seventyfour/GI; Guvendemir/GI; Jayson_Lys/GI; Sean Anthony Eddy/GI; SDI Productions/GI; Ryan Mcvay/GI; Klaus Vedfelt/GI

Key GI= Getty Images

We would like to thank the following reviewers for providing feedback on the draft manuscript: Wenlian Yang and Mosharraf Hossain.

> Contents

› How to use this book

This Workbook provides questions for you to practise what you have learned in class. There is a unit to match each unit in your Coursebook.

Tips to help you with your learning. ────────────────►

READING TIP

When you read a text, think about the purpose of the text and the intended audience.

Information to help you find out more about grammar. ───────────►

USE OF ENGLISH

Report: Making cities more sustainable

Recent urbanisation has resulted in cities that are congested and unmanageable. It is hoped that the recommendations made in this report will help to make cities more sustainable and resilient for the future. Reducing carbon footprint is considered to be a priority. Public transport systems should be improved in order to relieve traffic congestions and reduce commuter time. Pedestrian and car-free zones that encourage people to walk more would help to reduce air pollution. There are several other recommendations in this report which…

Check!

1 Impersonal language is often used in academic reports to make them sound more objective. Read the text and underline any impersonal language.

Notice

2 Which parts of the report extract above use the following?

   a A passive verb   ....

   b *It is* as the subject   ....

   c *There are* as the subject   ....

   d A complex noun as the subject   ....

Use the Cambridge Learner Corpus to get your grammar right! ────────────►

GET IT RIGHT!

Remember to think carefully about when an action started, whether a past action has a connection to the present, if an action continued over time or is routine.

There are opportunities to practise your grammar on the Use of English pages in each unit. Each Use of English lesson is divided into three parts:

Focus: These grammar questions help you to master the basics. ————▶

> ### Focus
> 3   **Circle the words that each reference word in bold refers to.**
>
> a   Most of my friends are online and I never actually meet **them** in person.
>
> b   I had a fight with my best friend and now **she** won't talk to me.
>
> c   My friends like chatting on text and message boards. I'm not keen on **it**.
>
> d   I spend a lot of time online and **this** has caused conflicts with my parents.
>
> e   Many people look at their phone before going to sleep. **This** can sometimes cause sleeping problems.

Practice: These grammar questions help you to become more accurate and confident. ————▶

> ### Practice
> 4   **Decide which sentences are unclear and rewrite them in your notebook.**
>
> a   My friends socialise on social media networks, but I'm not keen on them.
>
> b   The students make jokes about each other. They're really annoying.
>
> c   Eric had problems reading the instructions and they prevented him from understanding the task.
>
> d   After Rita had apologised to Simona, she promised always to be her best friend.

Challenge: These questions will help you use language fluently and prepare for the next level. ————▶

> ### Challenge
> 5   **Read this travel blog.**
>   **Complete the text with the correct form of** *used to* **or** *be / get used to.*
>
> Hi and welcome to my travel blog! I'm in the beautiful south of France where we are on a two-week cycling tour. This is day three, and so far we've covered about 60 km. I ___'m not used to cycling___ ....¹ (not, cycle) 20 km every day and my legs are seriously tired! We get up at dawn every morning (I ....² (get) up early amazingly fast, you'll be surprised to hear!) so we can get an early start while it is cool. We ....³ (come) to France for camping holidays when I was little, but we ....⁴ (not, go)

Questions that help you to think about your learning and progress. ————▶

> **REFLECTION**
>
> **Write answers to these questions in your notebook.**
>
> a   How has this unit widened your view of social inequality?
>
> b   List five key words or phrases that you associate with the topic of this unit. Why did you choose them?
>
> c   List three ways in which you think social inequality is changing.
>
> d   What kinds of inequality are there in your country? How can they be changed?
>
> e   List three positive things we can do in our daily lives to combat discrimination against others.

1 My generation

Think about it: Teenage choices

1   Read the questions. Then complete them using words from the box.

---
academic performance   career   degree
entry requirements   non-academic achievements   peers
scholarship   student loan   undergraduate

Applying for university: Frequently asked questions

Here are some of the most frequently asked questions about our college courses.
Don't see your question here? Write to us and we'll do our best to answer!

I   What are the .... for getting a place at university?

2   How long does it usually take to complete a ....?

3   Do all .... courses in science require an A level in maths?

4   How can I apply for a .... to help pay for my tuition fees?

5   Can anyone get a .... from a bank to pay for accommodation and living costs?

6   Are exam results and overall .... the most important criteria?

7   What about things like art and sport? Are .... also important?

8   How do I decide which subject to choose if I don't know my .... yet?

9   Will there be an opportunity to get the opinions of my .... who already attend the university?

2   **Write answers to the questions from Exercise 1 in your notebook using information about universities in your country.**

3   **Read the information. Then read the statements and write true, false or not given.**

Here at Watson University, we are proud to maintain the very highest standards of teaching and learning. Whatever type of degree you are applying for, we provide an ideal environment to develop your potential and enable you to achieve the career of your dreams. We've got one of the largest selections of undergraduate courses in the country. Entry requirements vary according to the department for which you are applying. To make the most of your time with us, we encourage all students to work together with their peers to create a collaborative and supportive environment. For students who may need financial support, we recommend applying for one of our scholarships or visiting our support centre for advice about how to get a student loan. For further information, search our course information by subject or department, or visit our FAQ page to contact us with your question.

a   The university prepares you for a specific job. ....

b   The university offers a wide range of BA courses. ....

c   Non-academic achievements are one of the entry requirements.

    ....

d   Students are encouraged to work alone. ....

e   You can borrow money from the university. ....

Challenge

4   **Write two more questions to add to the frequently asked questions in Exercise 1.**

    1   ....

    2   ....

5   **Write two questions to ask the university in Exercise 3.**

    1   ....

    2   ....

Psychology and medicine: Adolescence and the brain

1   Skim the extracts and match them with the type of text.
    Who is the intended audience for each text?

> advice article ....   book summary ....   dictionary ....   scientific article ....

a   **Circadian rhythm** – a term used to describe physical, mental and behavioural changes related to a 24-hour cycle. Sleeping at night and being awake during the day is one example of a circadian rhythm.

....

b   Providing a complete and concise account of the nervous system, this is the perfect resource for all students of neurobiology and provides a fascinating guide to **neurodevelopmental** processes and the understanding of **cognition** and knowledge acquisition.

....

READING TIP

When you read a text, think about the purpose of the text and the intended audience. This will help you to frame the information more easily and effectively.

c   Emotions are an important of a **natural adaptive biological process** in adolescence. Both positive and negative emotions are necessary for this development during **puberty** and are important for your teenager's growth and development into an adult. These emotions will eventually **stabilise** as your teen starts to mature. There is also some **causal data** to suggest that teens have a different circadian rhythm from adults.

....

d   Why and how the structure of **white matter** changes and develops across the human **lifespan** is the focus of this study. Compared with **grey matter**, the structure of white matter, which lies beneath the brain's surface and makes up half the human brain, has been far less frequently researched. Using new data from **MRI imaging**, this study aims to investigate a possible **correlation** between changes in white matter after doing regular physical activity and learning complex tasks.

....

2   Match the words in bold in the extracts with the definitions below.

   a   daily pattern of activity ....

   b   type of non-invasive diagnostic tool ....

   c   brain tissue beneath the surface of the brain ....

   d   brain tissue on the surface of the brain ....

   e   changes that occur as a result of evolutionary development ....

   f   results that prove that one thing is caused by another ....

g   processes of knowledge and perception in the brain ....

h   relating to the development of the brain and the nervous system ....

i   the length of time that a person lives ....

j   when certain attributes tend to occur together ....

k   to become firm or steady ....

l   when a child's body begins to develop and mature ....

3   **Read the article. Then complete the flowchart.**
     Choose no more than two words from the article for each answer.

Typical teenage circadian cycle

Melatonin is the naturally occurring hormone that is cyclically released as darkness approaches and prepares humans for sleep. In general, melatonin release follows approximately a 24-hour daily cycle, ideally ensuring consistent sleep patterns from day to day.

One change in the body during puberty is closely related to how you sleep. There is a shift in the timing of your circadian rhythms. Before puberty, your body makes you sleepy around 8 or 9 p.m. When puberty begins, this rhythm shifts a couple hours later. Despite getting up at 7 a.m., you may not feel fully awake until 9 or 10 a.m.

From 10 a.m. to 1 p.m., you will feel the highest point of energy of your day. Your body temperature rises and you will feel more alert. But the late night and disrupted sleep from the night before starts to kick in, and from 2 to 5 p.m. you may start to feel drowsy and long for a sugary snack or drink to stay awake.

Credit: NIGMS

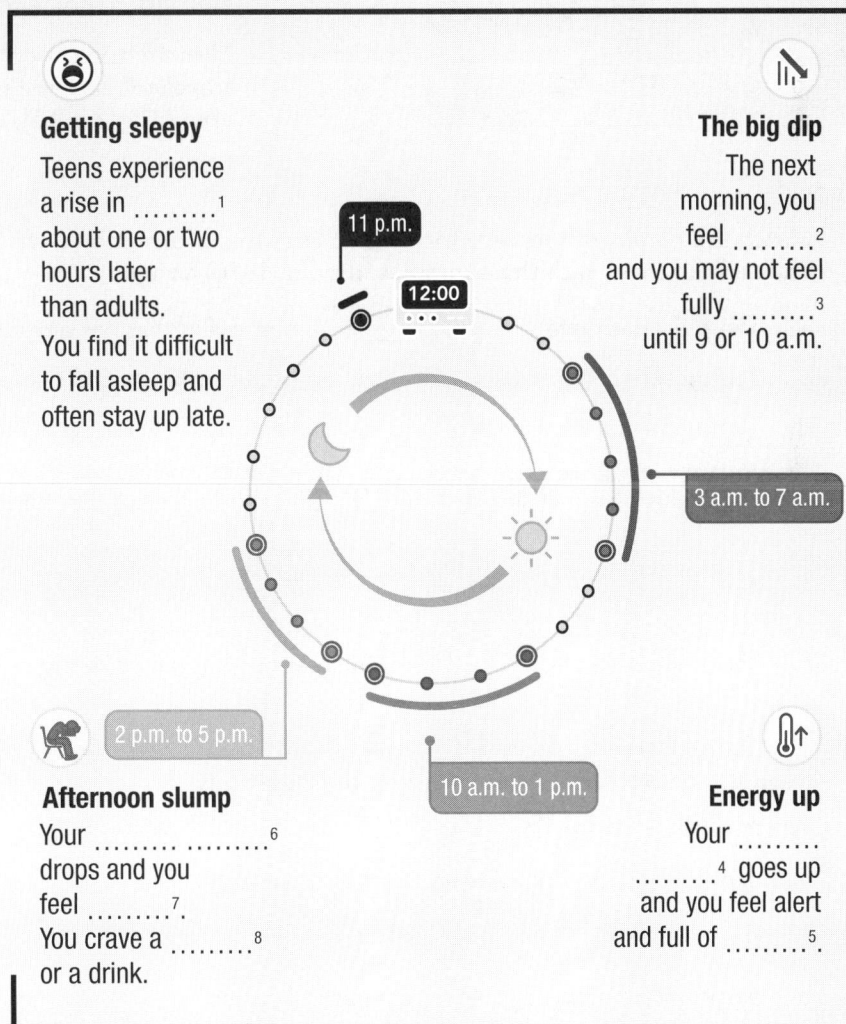

Getting sleepy
Teens experience a rise in ....[1] about one or two hours later than adults.
You find it difficult to fall asleep and often stay up late.

11 p.m.

12:00

The big dip
The next morning, you feel ....[2] and you may not feel fully ....[3] until 9 or 10 a.m.

3 a.m. to 7 a.m.

2 p.m. to 5 p.m.

10 a.m. to 1 p.m.

Afternoon slump
Your ....[6] drops and you feel ....[7].
You crave a ....[8] or a drink.

Energy up
Your ....[4] goes up and you feel alert and full of ....[5]

Use of English: Present, perfect and past forms

USE OF ENGLISH

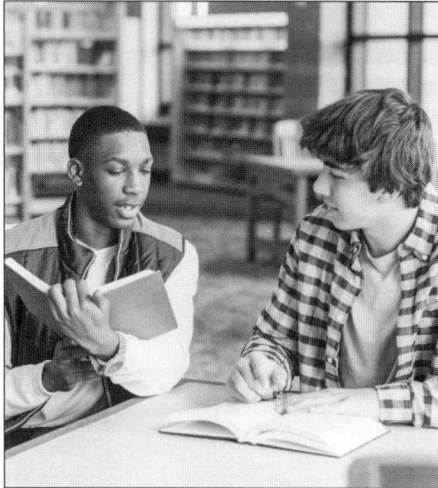

Adnan: Hi Johannes, what are your plans after finishing school?

Johannes: I've been applying[1] to different universities for next year. How about you?

Adnan: I've received[2] one offer of a place, but I want[3] to take a year off first.

Johannes: Really? What do your parents think[4] about that?

Adnan: They didn't like[5] the idea at first, but they're starting[6] to come round to it!

Johannes: My sister took[7] a gap year before going to uni and she travelled[8] all over Europe. She had never travelled[9] abroad before that, and she really enjoyed[10] it!

Check!

1   Match the names of the verb forms (a–f) with the information (i–vi) below.
Then match them with the examples in bold (1–10) above.

a   The present simple

b   The present continuous

c   The past simple

d   The present perfect simple

e   The present perfect continuous

f   The past perfect

i   a past event that has a result in the present ☐ ....

ii   a stative verb used to express an opinion ☐ ....

iii   an activity that started in the past and is still going on ....

iv   an action or event that happened in the past before another event ☐ ....

v   an event that happened in the past and is finished ☐ ....

vi   events that are currently in progress ....

Notice

2   Read the conversation again. Answer the questions.

Which verbs:

a   express a connection between past and present?

....

b   emphasise that an action or event hasn't finished?

....

Focus

3 Circle the correct verb form.

a We've already *completed / been completing* all our final exams.

b My parents *believe / are believing* that it's important to have a good career.

c He *had / has* studied several languages before he went to university.

d What *are you thinking / do you think* of doing next year?

e We have *changed / been changing* teachers three times this year!

f I *have been learning / learned* Japanese in school this year.

Practice

4 Four of these sentences are incorrect. Find the mistakes and correct them.

a They've been doing an online maths course this year.

b This is the first time I visit England.

c I am living here since last December.

d I wanted to visit the museum but I wasn't having enough time.

e I'm usually getting good marks for my English composition.

Challenge

5 Read the blog post. Complete the text with verbs from the box using the simple, continuous or perfect forms of the present or past.

| begin   get   help   join   live   not realise   take   visit |

Hi! My name is Jake and I'm from Tasmania, where I ....[1] with my parents. At the moment, I ....[2] my aunt in Melbourne for a few weeks. I ....[3] at a wildlife refuge for the last week. My aunt ....[4] the refuge a few months ago, and there are volunteers from all generations. For several months, they ....[5] care of animals that were injured in the forest fires. We ....[6] hundreds of koala bears to recover and get back to the wild. Before coming to Melbourne, I ....[7] the full impact of climate change on wildlife, but now I ....[8] to understand why it is so important for everyone to work together to protect the planet.

GET IT RIGHT!

Remember to think carefully about when an action started or finished, whether a past action has a connection to the present, whether an action continued over time or is a daily routine and whether the verb is stative or dynamic.

Examples:
We have travelled around the world for one year and are now in Nepal. (travel is an activity that continued over some time = have been travelling)

We aren't knowing each other very well yet. (know is a stative verb that doesn't use continuous form = don't know)

Use of English: Reference words

USE OF ENGLISH

Teen problems: I feel like none of my friends really like me. What can I do?

Friendships are incredibly important when we're growing up. **They** can help us feel more confident and help us to define who we are, so I can understand why **this feeling** is worrying you.

Friends are important, but it's also important to choose **them** wisely. Are **they** people you can trust? What is important for you in a friendship? Are **these values** also important to your friends? **This** is one way to decide who your true friends are.

A real friend is someone who you can turn to when you have problems. **These** might be related to issues around bullying or negative feelings about yourself. If you can talk to them about your problems, **it** is one step towards true friendship.

Check!

1   Read the advice about friendship. What do the words in bold refer to?

   a   they   friendships.....................

   b   this feeling ....

   c   them ....

   d   they ....

   e   these values ....

   f   this ....

   g   these ....

   h   it ....

Notice

2   Read the letter again. Match the questions below with the words in Exercise 1. Write the correct letter next to each question.

   a   Which words refer to a single previous noun? ....

   b   Which ones refer to some previous ideas? ....

   c   Which words refer to a noun within the same sentence? ....

   d   Which ones refer to something in a previous sentence? ....

   e   Which examples use a synonym or a paraphrase of a previous word or idea? ....

Focus

3 **Circle the words that each reference word in bold refers to.**

a Most of my friends are online and I never actually meet **them** in person.

b I had a fight with my best friend and now **she** won't talk to me.

c My friends like chatting on text and message boards. I'm not keen on **it**.

d I spend a lot of time online and **this** has caused conflicts with my parents.

e Many people look at their phone before going to sleep. **This** can sometimes cause sleeping problems.

Practice

4 **Decide which sentences are unclear and rewrite them in your notebook.**

a My friends socialise on social media networks, but I'm not keen on them.

b The students make jokes about each other. They're really annoying.

c Eric had problems reading the instructions and they prevented him from understanding the task.

d After Rita had apologised to Simona, she promised always to be her best friend.

Challenge

5 **Read the extract from an essay. Complete the text with words from the box.**

them	these	these	this	this	them

ARE ONLINE FRIENDSHIPS AS GOOD AS IN-PERSON FRIENDSHIPS?

On the one hand, it is true that making friends online is easier and faster than meeting friends in person. ....¹ is one reason why many teenagers have lots of friends on different social media platforms. For ....² young people, chatting and texting online is just as natural as meeting up for a coffee. You can also meet a wide variety of people who share your interests. ....³ means you can more easily meet people who are compatible with you.

On the other hand, one disadvantage of ....⁴ friendships is that you can have too many friends, and you don't have time to keep up with all of ....⁵. Messaging can also lead to misunderstandings in texts, and it's not always easy to resolve ....⁶.

6 Read one of your essays and underline all the reference words. Could you add any? Are any of them ambiguous?

LANGUAGE TIP

Vague pronoun reference

Sometimes it is unclear what the reference words refer to and the reader may be confused.

Example: *I think some students are sending bullying emails but I'm afraid to report* **them**. (It isn't clear whether them refers to students or emails.)

To make this clearer, you can replace the pronoun with a synonym:

I think my classmates are sending bullying emails but I'm afraid to report ***their messages.***

Academic writing: A discussion essay

1 These are some useful words for presenting different views on a topic. Complete the sentences with words from the box.

| agree | argued | believe | evident | extent | hand | other | view |

a It could be .... that young children should not use computers at an early age.

b On the one ...., there are some advantages to having older siblings.

c On the .... hand, some children can feel they don't get enough attention.

d It is difficult to .... how many students experience bullying online.

e Having longer school holidays may be beneficial to a certain

....

f It is true that social media is an important way for people to stay in touch.

This is .... in the amount of time they spend on their phones.

g I would .... that many students are motivated by learning online.

h Some people hold the .... that young people should have more free time and less homework.

> **WRITING TIP**
>
> **Writing a discussion essay**
>
> A discussion essay question asks you to set out the two sides of a specific issue. You will be expected to present arguments for each side of the issue equally, with evidence to support each one. Then state your own opinion in the conclusion.

2 Read the essay question. Which response agrees or disagrees with the question? Then write your opinion in one sentence.

Some people think that young people today are much more used to using technology than previous generations and that that is why there is a communication gap between younger and older generations. Others believe that communication between the generations has always been more challenging. Discuss both sides of the question and give your opinion.

a Communicating on social media is so different nowadays, so it is not surprising that older and younger people find it difficult to communicate. ....

b Younger and older generations communicate in different ways, but it's not because of technology. ....

Your opinion: ....

3   **Read the essay question. Then copy and complete the graphic organiser with your ideas about the topic. Consider the questions in the box to help you.**

All parents want their children to have a successful future. Some people think that schools should teach life skills, such as planning a budget or developing self-esteem. Others believe that only academic subjects that help students to pass exams should be taught. Discuss both sides of the issue and give your opinion.

How do we know what life skills are going to be useful in the future?	Who will teach life skills to students if they don't learn them at school?
Will students be motivated to learn life skills or will they think it is a waste of time?	Will teaching life skills take up valuable time that could be spent on exam preparation?
Are life skills something students can learn on their own?	

For ← Teaching life skills at schools → Against

WRITING TIP

Do:
- provide examples and explanations
- use signpost phrases to connect your ideas
- use reference words to create a cohesive text.

Don't:
- use informal language
- include irrelevant information
- stray from the main topic.

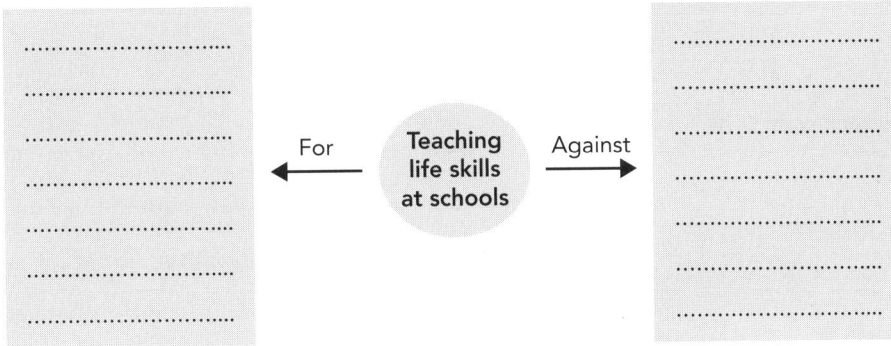

4   **Now decide your opinion and choose one of these statements for your conclusion to the essay question in Exercise 3. Complete the conclusion with your main idea.**

a   Although learning a range of academic subjects is important for students, I feel that ....
....

b   Although learning life skills is important for students, I think it is more important for them to ....
....

5   **Write the rest of your essay in your notebook. Remember to use academic language for discussing both sides of a topic.**

Check your progress

Vocabulary

1 **Circle the correct answers.**

a Students with high grades can sometimes apply for a .... to help pay their college fees.

   A scholarship

   B career

   C qualification

b Students who are the same age and level as you are your ....

   A colleagues

   B peers

   C partners

c If you take out a loan, it means that you .... money.

   A give

   B lend

   C borrow

d Good exam results at school are usually part of the college entry ....

   A achievements

   B requirements

   C performance

e White and grey matter are two types of .... in the brain.

   A cell

   B tissue

   C nerve

f An MRI is a type of ....

   A treatment

   B diagnosis

   C diagnostic tool

g Behaviour that is affected by daylight is known as the circadian ....

   A rhythm

   B circle

   C pattern

h Puberty is the time of life between the ages of ....

   A 5 and 10

   B 8 and 12

   C 8 and 14

Grammar

2 **Circle the correct words to complete the text.**

I *'m thinking / think*[1] of going to college next year. So far I *'ve been visiting / have visited*[2] three different colleges. Most of them *are having / have*[3] regular open days for school students and their parents to come and look around. On our last visit, a university student *has led / was leading*[4] the tour and *showed / was showing*[5] us the library, the computer centre and the student cafeteria. I think you're expected to be quite independent at uni and *this / they*[6] means that you need to be very motivated and not rely on the teachers too much. *They / These*[7] can help you if you have a specific question, but you can also go to the academic support centre for more general issues. *These / This*[8] can range from help with academic study skills to managing your budget.

Reading

3 Skim the paragraph and decide who the intended audience is.

The human brain starts to develop before birth and continues developing throughout childhood and adolescence into adulthood. The rate of brain development is not consistent over this period of time – it varies greatly according to the individual and their environment. Therefore, it is unrealistic to expect all children to develop at the same rate all the time or at the same pace as their peers. By developing strategies for offering flexibility and accommodating variability, we can facilitate better brain development for all children.

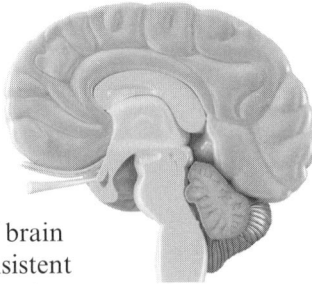

This extract is from an article for:

A teachers and educators

B doctors and brain surgeons

C health and nutrition experts

4 Which statement best corresponds with the ideas in the text in Exercise 3?

A We should consider carefully how to evaluate each child's development.

B We should not have unrealistic expectations of children's brain development.

C Brain development should be included in the school curriculum.

Speaking

5 Use phrases from the box to write your responses to the questions in your notebook.

> As far as I'm concerned
>
> From my point of view
>
> I'd definitely / probably say that
>
> There's no doubt in my mind

a Do you think academic performance is more important than non-academic achievements, or are they both equally important?

b Do you think it is important to study the brain? How can such studies help us?

c How important are friendships in your life? What in your opinion makes a good friendship?

Writing

6 Read the essay question and underline the key words. Write a plan for a discussion essay in your notebook.

Some parents send their children to after school classes to help them improve their exam grades. Other parents think that children should enjoy their free time with their friends. Discuss both views and give your opinion.

REFLECTION

Write answers to these questions in your notebook.

a How did you go about learning and remembering new vocabulary items from this unit? Which method do you feel worked the best?

b Which grammar points in this unit do you feel you need to study more carefully? How could you study them?

c How easy was it for you to decide your opinion of topics in this unit? Which topic was most difficult to express an opinion about? Why?

d How did you write your notes when planning your ideas for an essay? Think of three different ways you could lay out your ideas in your notebook.

e What did you learn about collaborating with others through your work in this unit? What did you do well?

2 Travel: Help or hindrance?

Think about it: Tourism and the environment

1 **Read the holiday descriptions. Complete them using words in the box.**
Which types of holiday would you be interested in trying?

aviation	biodegradable	carbon emissions	community	erosion	extreme tourism
mountain ranges	mountaineering	poverty	remote	sewage	sustainable	trekking	waste

☐ We want to go trekking............¹ in the Amazon rainforest next year. We're staying in an eco-lodge that uses energy from solar panels, so it's completely ....².All profits benefit the local ....³, which helps to reduce ....⁴.

☐ We're going on a canal boat holiday this year. Years ago, this canal was heavily polluted by industrial ....⁵ from factories and ....⁶ from the nearby town. But now it has been cleaned up and as a result, the fish and wildlife have gradually returned.

☐ I've been ....⁷ for several years, and this year I've decided to challenge myself by climbing five peaks in five different ....⁸ around the world. I suppose it's a kind of ....⁹.

☐ We're going to volunteer with an environmental group this summer, picking up ....¹⁰ from the riverbanks and planting trees to prevent ....¹¹.

☐ We're going camping this summer. We decided to reduce our ....¹² by cycling, instead of driving, and taking only ....¹³ packaging with us for our food.

☐ I've decided not to travel long distances by plane any more. ....¹⁴ is responsible for so much air pollution. I don't think it's good for tourists to visit ....¹⁵ places.

2   Which of the holidays described in Exercise 1 do you think are best for the
    environment? Rank them in order from best (1) to worst (6) and write a number
    next to each one. Then explain your criteria.

    My criteria: ....

    ....

3   The words trip, travel and journey are easily confused.
    Circle the correct word to complete each sentence.

    a   I visited Hokkaido on my recent *travel /* (*trip*) to Japan.

    b   You can *travel / journey* by train from London to Paris.

    c   He went on a business *trip / journey* to Cairo.

    d   I'm planning to *travel / trip* to Mexico next year.

    e   The *trip / travel* takes about five hours.

    f   I want to go on a *travel / trip* around the world one day.

4   Read part of a lecture about eco-tourism.
    Write notes using key words and abbreviations.

    > Today we're going to talk about the concept of eco-tourism. Is there a way to
    > make tourism more sustainable and reduce its environmental impact? Rather
    > than giving up tourism altogether, which could have a negative economic
    > impact on communities, can eco-tourism offer tourism that is environmentally
    > sustainable? One idea might be to rethink your type of accommodation, for
    > example staying with host families or choosing accommodation that uses
    > renewable energy. Instead of opting for swimming pools and golf courses,
    > choose low-impact activities such as trekking or cycling, or take part in activity
    > holidays that help conserve and protect the environment.

    Title: ....

    Topic: ....

    1   ....

    2   ....

Challenge

5   Think of a popular tourist destination in your country and say how tourism has
    helped or hindered the economy and the life of the community in that place.
    Write a paragraph in your notebook.

Geography: Tourism in the Galápagos Islands

1 Read the article. Then match headings a–g to the correct paragraphs (1–5). Two headings are not needed.

a Steps taken to protect the islands ....

b History and background of the islands ....

c Development of tourism ....

d Positive impacts of tourism ....

e Reasons why this is a popular tourist destination ....

f Negative impacts of tourism ....

g Effects of climate change on the ecosystem ....

Tourism in the Galápagos Islands

*The Galápagos Islands have become a popular destination for thousands of tourists, but has tourism helped the islands or has it hindered the conservation of its unique **flora** and **fauna**?*

1 Spectacular volcanic peaks, white sandy beaches, sparkling azure waters – it's hard to imagine a more beautiful travel destination than the Galápagos Islands. For hundreds of years, the wildlife and flora developed here in isolation. As a result, it is now home to hundreds of unique species such as the blue-footed booby and the marine iguana. And many of the animals are unafraid of humans – imagine swimming with giant sea turtles or sitting next to a sea lion for a selfie! The experience is a magnet for nature lovers, birdwatchers and scientists alike.

2 Located over 1000 km from the mainland of Ecuador, the **archipelago** consists of over a hundred islands that cover an area of 45,000 sq km. The islands were discovered by Europeans in 1535, but because of the unfertile terrain no one lived there until the 1800s, when settlers went there and started fishing and farming.

3 What started in the 1960s with small groups of tourists arriving by boat has now become a major industry. There are two airports and the number of tourists has increased dramatically from 6,000 to well over 200,000 per year. More people have moved there for employment opportunities as well. Whereas in the 1960s the local population was about 3,000, it is now closer to 30,000. The tourist industry forms a vital part of the economy and provides significant revenue for the government of Ecuador.

4   Inevitably, the increase in tourism has created stress on the environment. Not only does the movement and noise distress wildlife, there is also water pollution from waste and air pollution from traffic. Recently, activity holidays such as horse-riding and scuba diving have become popular, and these too can have a high impact. Another danger is the importation of invasive species; ants and wasps, for example, have been introduced along with imported foods.

5   To protect **biodiversity** and the fragile **ecosystem**, the area has been declared a marine reserve and a UNESCO World Heritage Site. Only the four largest islands are inhabited. 97 per cent of the islands are protected and no housing or hotels can be built there. Access is restricted to specific sites only when accompanied by a certified guide. All tourists have to pay a fee of $100 towards the cost of **conservation**. Tourists can also help by choosing environment friendly accommodation and tours, and by behaving responsibly.

---

archipelago: a group of small islands

biodiversity: variety of types of animals and plants

conservation: protecting natural environments

ecosystem: interdependence of living things in a specific area

fauna: animals

flora: plants

---

2   **Which of these is the best concluding sentence for the article in Exercise 1?**

   A   Everyone has to work together to ensure the survival of this island paradise.

   B   Further restrictions are likely to be introduced in future to protect the islands.

   C   Tourism is likely to increase and will provide more revenue for conservation work.

3   **What are each of these an example of?**

   a   blue-footed booby   *Animals that are unique to the Galápagos Islands*

   b   giant sea turtles   ....

   c   ants   ....

   d   airports   ....

   e   horse-riding   ....

> **READING TIP**
>
> When you read an article that gives examples to support a main idea, try to evaluate why the writer has chosen those examples and what they are intended to show.

Challenge

4   **Read the article in Exercise 1 again. Answer these questions in your notebook.**

   a   Would you like to visit these islands? Why or why not?

   b   What further steps could be taken to conserve the islands?

   c   What do you predict for the future of these islands?

Use of English: Modals of obligation (*should*, *must* and *have to*)

USE OF ENGLISH

The ancient city of Machu Picchu

To conserve the amazing heritage of this historic archaeological site, there are some rules:

- You must keep to the trails.
- You mustn't climb or lean on walls.
- You have to stay in a group accompanied by the official tour guide.
- You should carry the minimum number of bags or luggage.
- You shouldn't take photos using a selfie stick.
- You don't have to wear special shoes, but you shouldn't wear shoes with hard soles.

Check!

1 Underline the modals of obligation in the rules above.
What do you think are the reasons for each of these rules?

....

....

Notice

2 **Match the modals with the rules.**

Which modal verb(s)…

a is followed by an infinitive? ....

b don't use *do* to form a negative? ....

c express obligation? ....

d expresses prohibition? ....

e express recommendation? ....

f expresses lack of obligation? ....

Focus

3   Complete the sentences with the correct modal verb.

a   Visitors .... bring large amounts of food, only snacks are recommended.

b   You .... bring in plastic water bottles. They are banned.

c   You .... book your tickets in advance because they sell out quickly.

d   Everyone .... be accompanied by a tour guide. You can't walk alone.

e   Tourists .... to take the bus; they can also hike up the mountain.

Practice

4   Correct the mistake in each of these sentences.

a   The tour was sold out so we ~~must~~ come back the following day.
        had to
        ^

b   You haven't to buy the audio guide. It's not essential.

c   We had an excellent guidebook, so we hadn't to join the guided tour.

d   It suddenly started to rain so we must buy an umbrella.

e   We were able to reuse our ticket. We hadn't to buy a new ticket.

Challenge

5   Read the rules for visiting Yellowstone National Park. Complete the sentences with a reason for each rule.

a   It's not a good idea to go off the marked trails. *You shouldn't go off the marked trails because you might get lost.*

b   Don't feed the wild animals. ....

c   Set up camp in designated areas only. ....

d   Don't swim in the hot springs. ....

e   No need to book meals in a restaurant. Bring a picnic. ....

f   Bring a rain jacket and warm clothes for cooler weather. ....

> ### GET IT RIGHT!
>
> Remember that we use *mustn't* to express prohibition, that is, something which is not allowed. We use *don't have to* for absence of obligation, that is, something which isn't necessary. Notice that *must* for obligation has no past tense. Use *had to* instead.
>
> Examples:
> *This exhibition is free. You **don't have to** pay anything.* (not *mustn't*)
>
> *There were so many tourists at the museum yesterday that we **had to** wait a long time to get in.* (not *must*)

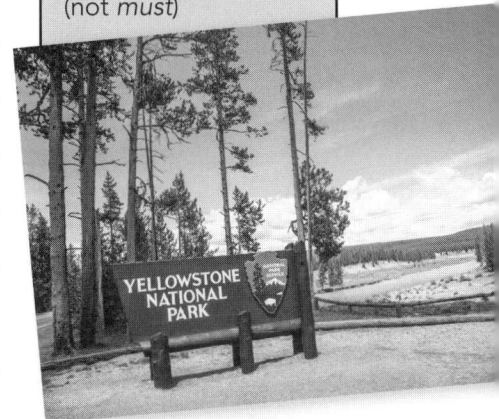

Use of English: *used to, be used to, get used to*

USE OF ENGLISH

Q: How has tourism changed in the last ten years?

A: Tourism has changed a lot in the last decade. Ten years ago, people used to book their holidays through a travel agent. Nowadays, we're used to booking flights and hotels online. In the past, people didn't use to take many photos because they were expensive to develop. Nowadays, everyone is used to taking hundreds of photos and sharing them online. People often took lots of short holidays, because flights were cheap, but now we're starting to get used to holidays that are more sustainable and kinder to the environment.

Check!

1 Read the information above about tourism. Underline all the examples of *used to*. Which examples refer to the past and which to the present?

Past: ....

....

Present: ....

....

Notice

2 In the examples you found in Exercise 1, which ones...

a use the verb *be*   ....

b use the verb *get*   ....

c use *use to* without a 'd' ....

d are followed by a verb   ....

Focus

3 Circle the correct words to complete each sentence.

a Nowadays, people *used to* / *are used to* getting the latest travel information online.

b Everyone has to *be used* / *get used* to reducing their carbon footprint when they travel.

c Tourists are *use to / used to* planning their own unique adventures by researching online.

d Did you *use / used* to travel a lot when you were a young child?

e People didn't *use / used* to know about the more remote travel destinations.

Practice

4 Correct the mistake in each sentence.

a We're used to ~~read~~ reading travel blogs to get ideas for our holidays.

b People didn't used to thinking about the environmental impact of their travel.

c We will have to get used to take the train instead of a plane.

d They didn't used to seeing so many tourists in their village.

e Tourists are getting used to be more adventurous in their travel choices.

Challenge

5 Read this travel blog.
Complete the text with the correct form of *used to* or *be / get used to*.

Hi and welcome to my travel blog! I'm in the beautiful south of France where we are on a two-week cycling tour. This is day three, and so far we've covered about 60 km. I 'm not used to cycling ....¹ (not, cycle) 20 km every day and my legs are seriously tired! We get up at dawn every morning (I ....² (get) up early amazingly fast, you'll be surprised to hear!) so we can get an early start while it is cool. We ....³ (come) to France for camping holidays when I was little, but we ....⁴ (not, go) anywhere too far from the coast. At the end of each day, we set up our tents and make a fire to cook dinner. At first it was hard after a full day's cycling, but I ....⁵ (totally) it now! But one thing I'll ....⁶ (never) is how quiet it is at night. Living in a big city, I ....⁷ (have) lots of noise around me day and night, so the complete silence is something new for me.

6 Think of three more ways that tourism has changed over the last decade.
Write sentences in your notebook using *used to*, *be used to* or *get used to*.

GET IT RIGHT!

Remember that when we talk about a past habit or state, *used to* is followed by a verb, not a gerund. We can use a gerund or a noun after *be/get used to*.

Examples: *People **used to send** postcards when they were on holiday.* (not *were used to sending*)

*We**'re used to posting** our photos instantly online.* (not *are used to post*)

Academic writing: A problem and solution essay

1 Underline phrases for expressing cause and effect in a–f. Then match the beginning of each sentence with its end from i–vi.

a Walking routes around the ancient city are overcrowded due to

b As a result of so many people crowding into the buildings

c Tourists sometimes sit or lean on walls which causes

d Walls are starting to disintegrate because of

e On account of tourists sharing selfies online

f Ticket prices have risen as a consequence of

i increased maintenance costs.

ii deterioration of the ancient structures.

iii more people are visiting remote parts of the site.

iv the huge popularity of the site.

v tourists leaning or standing on them.

vi doorways and steps have become damaged.

> **WRITING TIP**
>
> In a problem and solution essay, it is a good idea to choose two or three problems for which you can provide good examples and supporting details. Your introduction could paraphrase the question and outline the organisation of your essay.

2 Read the essay question. Then copy and complete the graphic organiser with your ideas about the topic. Consider the points in the box to help you.

Large numbers of tourists visit famous historic sites every year. The entry fees paid by visitors help to pay for conservation. On the other hand, large numbers of tourists can cause damage to the site. What problems do you think tourists cause and what are some possible solutions that will make visiting the site more sustainable?

> **STUDY TIP**
>
> **Brainstorming ideas**
>
> Before you start writing, read the question carefully and underline the key words. Brainstorm at least six ideas. Then choose the best three.

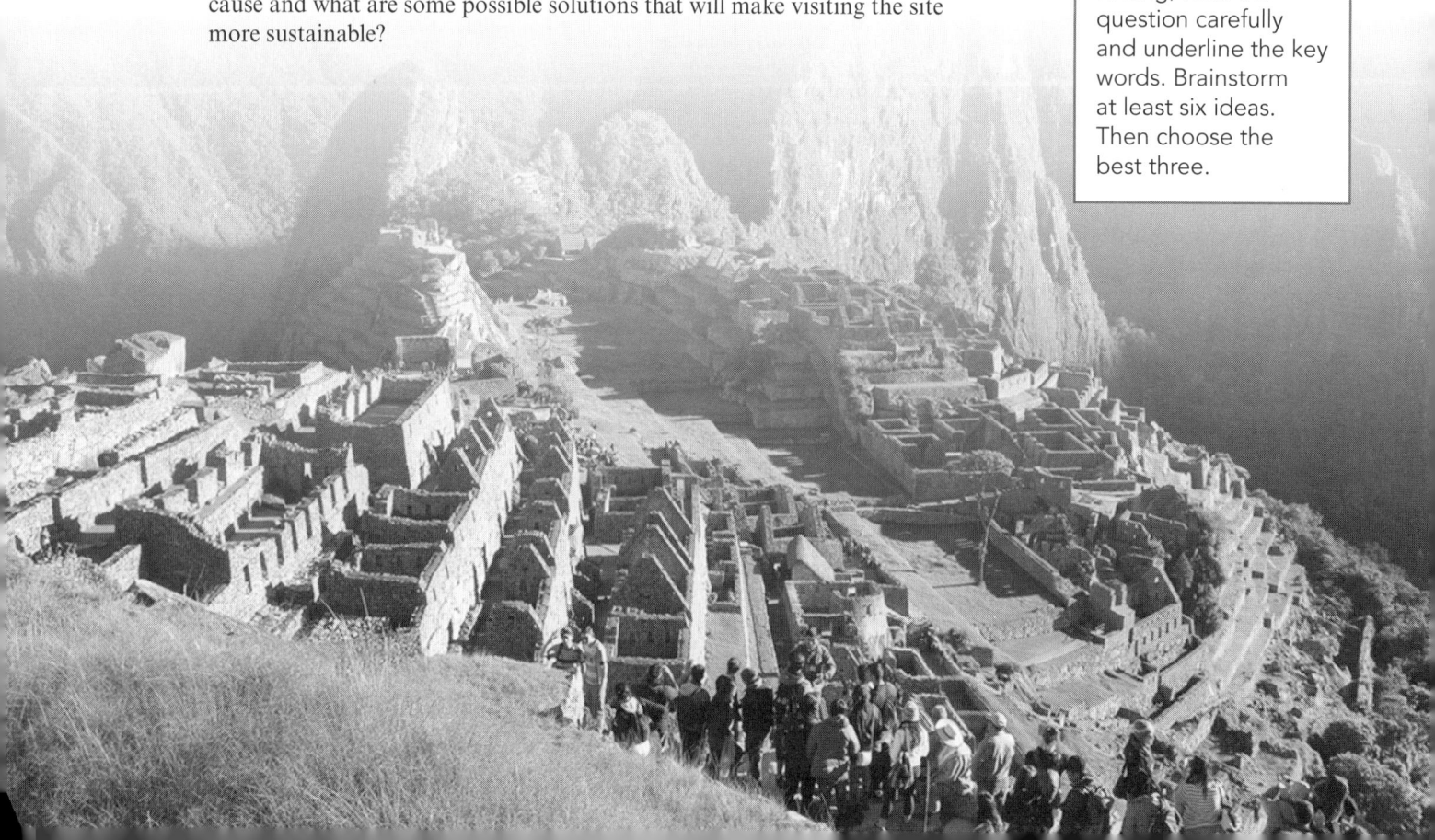

Problems	Solutions
overcrowding	higher ticket prices
....	....
....	....

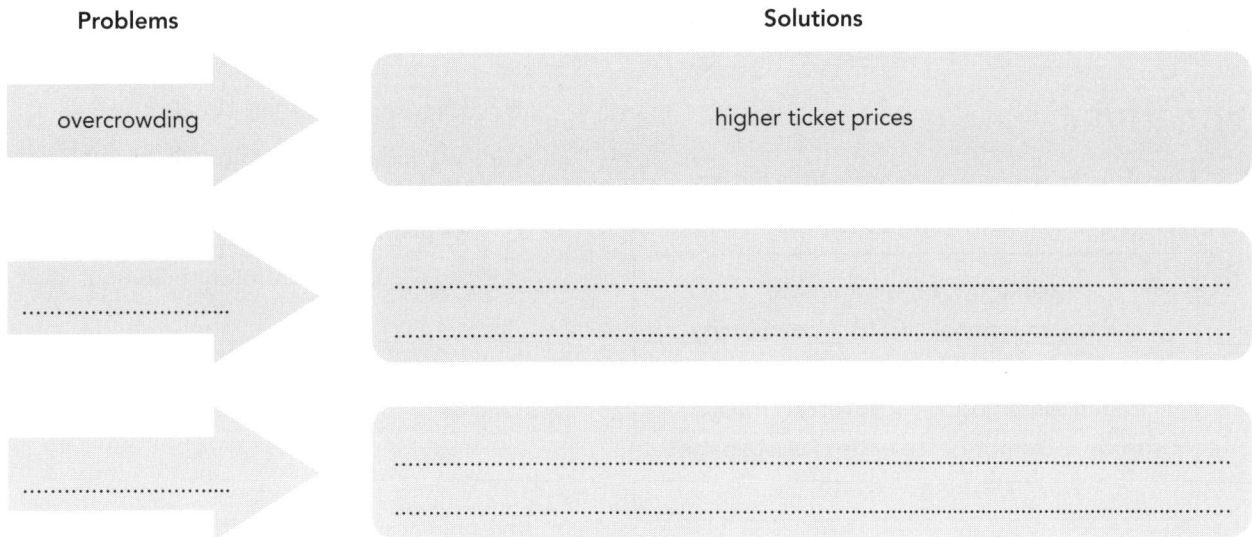

3   Tick the best topic sentence for each paragraph of your essay.

Paragraph A

☐ 1   Large numbers of tourists visit famous historic sites every year.

☐ 2   Many historic sites are endangered by the large numbers of tourists who visit them.

Paragraph B

☐ 1   Large numbers of tourists can cause a number of different problems for the conservation of the site.

☐ 2   Pompeii is an example of a historic site that is visited by thousands of tourists every year.

Paragraph C

☐ 1   Many ancient historic sites have taken steps to deal with these problems.

☐ 2   Tourists have caused a great deal of damage to ancient sites.

Paragraph D

☐ 1   In conclusion, we need to think about this problem more carefully.

☐ 2   In conclusion, it is essential to find ways of managing tourism so that it is less harmful.

**4   Write an essay answering the question in Exercise 2 in your notebook.
Remember to use academic language for expressing your opinion.**

> **WRITING TIP**
>
> **Do:**
> - provide examples and supporting details
> - use sequence words to signpost your ideas
> - make sure all your points are relevant to the essay question.
>
> **Don't:**
> - repeat the essay question word for word
> - give your opinion
> - make a list of problems.

Check your progress

Vocabulary

1   Complete the sentences with words from the box. There are seven extra words.

> aviation   biodegradable
> carbon emissions   GDP   community
> emitters   erosion   extreme
> mountaineering   poverty   range
> refuse   remote   sewage   sustainable
> trekking   waste

a   Skiing to the South Pole or diving in underground caves are examples of
    extreme .... tourism.

b   Tourism plays a big part in many economies and helps to boost the ....
    of countries.

c   The Himalayas are a mountain .... that has become popular with climbers.

d   Instead of plastic, try to use cardboard or paper packaging that is ....

e   Too many tourists walking through a site can wear down the paths and cause
    ....

f   Staying in a locally owned guest house or hotel can provide revenue for the local
    ....

g   Tourists are looking for ways to travel that are eco-friendly and more ....

h   It's best to hire a local guide if you go .... through the rainforest.

i   Airplanes are one of the biggest .... of air pollution.

j   Tourism can provide employment and help lift communities out of ....

Grammar

2   Circle the correct words to complete the sentences.

a   The hotel gets very busy in the summer, so you *should* / *must* book in advance.

b   I *am not used* / *didn't use* to travelling by plane. I prefer trains.

c   You *should* / *have to* get a visa if you're travelling to the US.

d   Our train was on time so we *hadn't* / *didn't have* to wait long at the station.

e   We *used to go* / *were used to going* abroad every year, but this year we're going somewhere local.

f   You *mustn't* / *don't have to* bring any skis or boots because you can rent skiing gear at the resort.

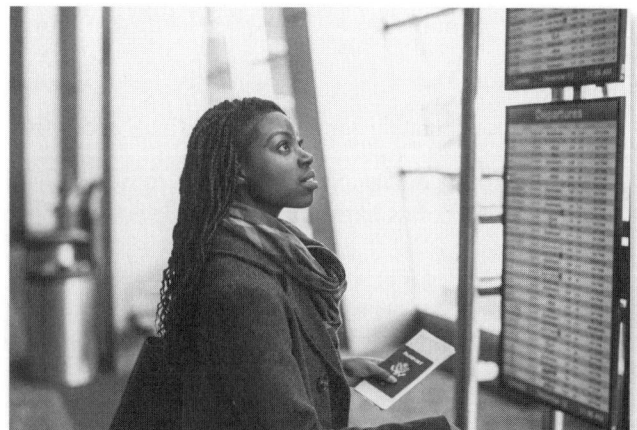

Reading

3 **Skim the paragraph and choose the best title.**

   A Is sustainable tourism possible?

   B Why do we need tourism?

   C What are the effects of tourism?

> Tourism is an industry that plays a vital role in many economies around the world. Many communities depend on tourism for employment and revenue. Recently, however, some places have started to experience the negative effects of too much tourism. Not only is excessive air travel a major contributor to carbon emissions, but popular tourist resorts with large hotels, for example, swimming pools and golf courses, require vast quantities of resources and often damage the local eco-system with water pollution from waste and sewage. Some have suggested sustainable tourism as a viable alternative. Travelling to less popular destinations, avoiding peak times, choosing local guest houses or tour companies are just a few examples. Others say that long-haul trips should be restricted or incur a heavy tax to discourage tourists from travelling long distances.

4 **What are these examples used to illustrate?**

   a employment

       ....

   b golf courses

       ....

   c local guest houses

       ....

   d tax

       ....

Writing

5 **Read the essay question and underline the key words. Write an introduction by paraphrasing the question and outlining your essay. Then continue the essay in your notebook.**

Many tour companies offer safari tours to see animals in the wild. What problems are associated with this type of tourism and what are some possible solutions?

....

....

....

....

....

....

....

....

REFLECTION

Write answers to these questions in your notebook.

a Choose five key words from this unit and write the definitions. Compare them with a dictionary

b Write three sentences to describe your holidays when you were younger. How are they different now? Use *used to or be/get used to*.

c Make a list of six rules in your local park, museum or nature reserve. Use modal verbs of obligation and prohibition.

d What are the key issues from this unit that you feel are most important? Have you changed your opinion about any of them?

e What did you improve in your speaking and writing skills in this unit? What did you do well?

3 Food choices

Think about it: The food we eat

1   Read the questions. Complete them with words from the box.

> absorb   cholesterol   dairy products   diagnosed   edible   food waste
> gluten   intestine   landfill   nutrients   protein   pulses

Send us your diet and nutrition questions. We'll do our best to answer them!

a   I can't eat ……………………. like cheese and yogurt. What can I use instead?

b   Which foods are good for encouraging beneficial bacteria in your …………………….?

c   Why are ……………………. like lentils and beans supposed to be healthy?
How long do they need to be cooked to be …………………….?

d   I'm allergic to ……………………., so I can't eat anything containing wheat-based flour,
but I love cakes and biscuits. Can you suggest some good alternatives for me?

e   I want to switch to a vegetarian diet, but I'm worried about not getting enough
……………………., which I usually get from meat. What foods should I eat to stay healthy?

f   I read that there is too much ……………………. in our ……………………. sites and
it causes methane gas, which is a pollutant. What can I do to reduce it?

g   Is it true that some foods like oats make it difficult for your stomach to …………………….
……………………. into your system? How can this be prevented?

h   I have been ……………………. with high ……………………. levels in my blood.
What types of can food help to lower them?

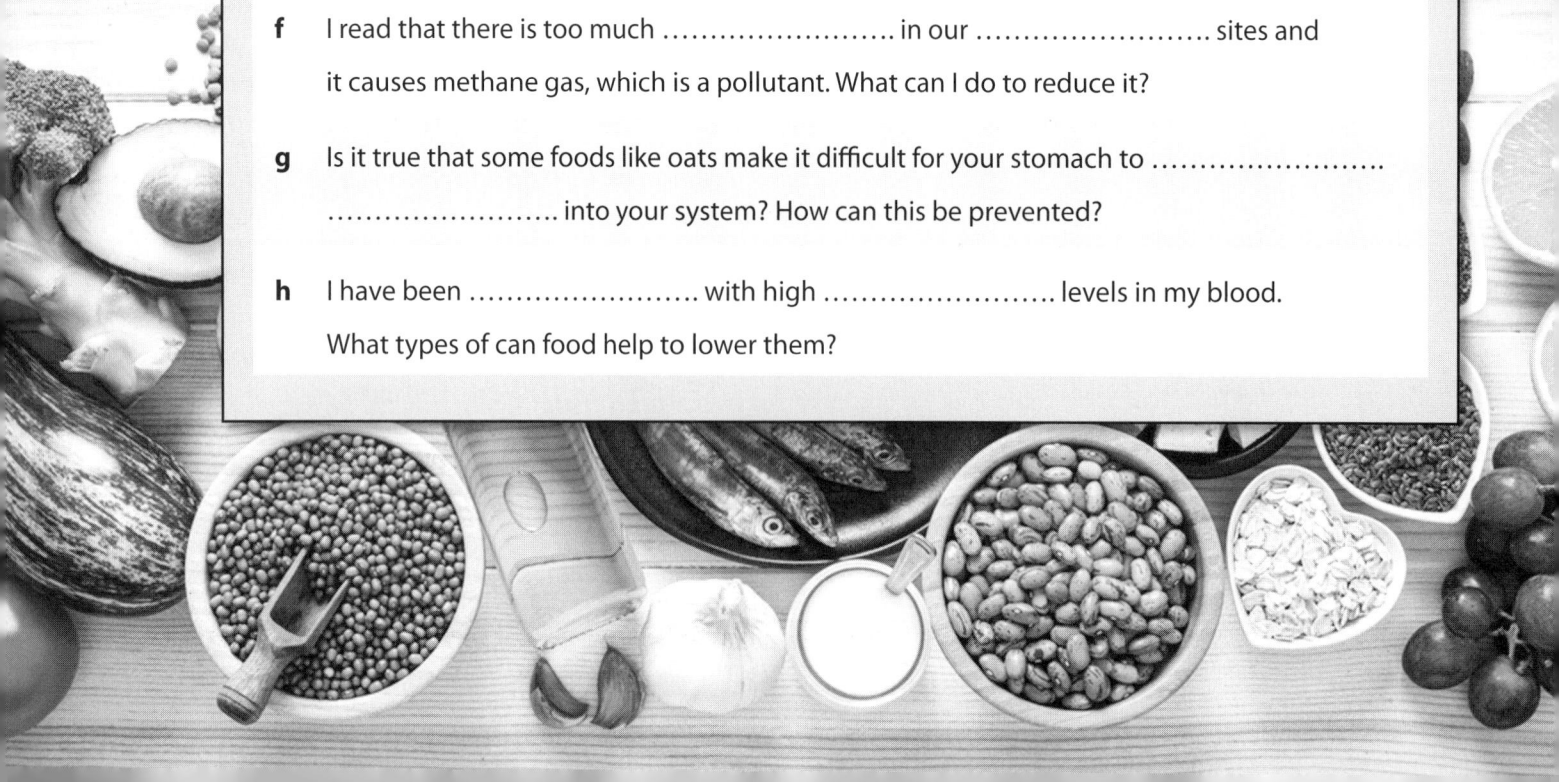

2   Circle the odd one out in each list. Say why it is different using a word from the box.

cholesterol   dairy   edible   legume   meat

a   cheese, milk, yoghurt, soy milk

....

b   burger, tofu, lamb, chicken

....

c   rice, lentils, peas, beans

....

d   potato skins, eggshells, stale bread, bean sprouts

....

e   meat, milk, butter, oats

....

Challenge

3   Answer these questions about your diet. Then write a paragraph in your notebook describing your typical daily diet. Say whether it is healthy or how it could be healthier.

a   What kind of dairy foods do you frequently eat or drink?

b   Do you often eat foods that are high in cholesterol?

c   What pulses do you eat regularly?

d   How often do you eat protein-rich foods?

e   What nutrients do you need more of in your diet?

f   Do you have any food allergies?

Food science and chemistry: The taste of chemistry

1 Look at the photo. Answer the questions.

a What do you know about how pickles are made?

....

....

b How many kinds of fermented foods can you think of?

....

....

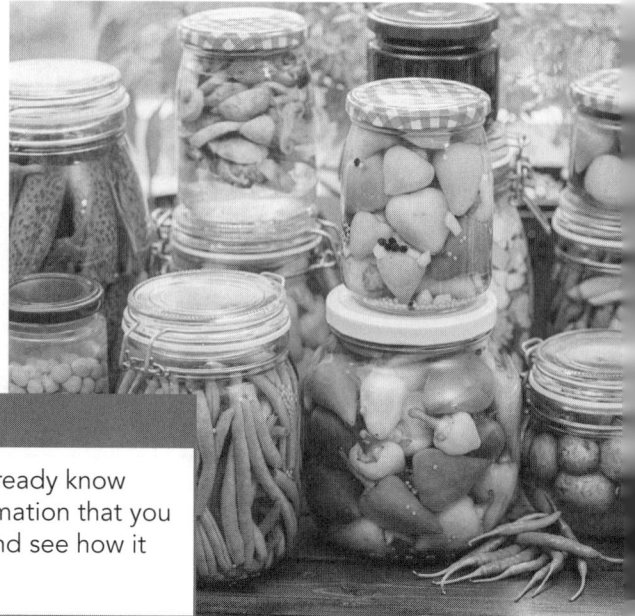

> ### READING TIP
>
> Before you start reading, it is helpful to think about what you already know about the topic. Ask yourself questions and identify some information that you don't know. This will help you to understand new information and see how it fits in with your existing knowledge.

2 Read the article. Underline the parts that are new information for you. Check your answers to Exercise 1.

The science of pickled and fermented food

Pickling and fermenting are two methods used to preserve vegetables so that they taste good and are safe to eat. Although there are some similarities between them, there are also some significant differences.

Pickling is the process of submerging vegetables such as cucumbers or onions in a mixture of salt and water or vinegar. The flavour of the vegetables changes during this process and becomes sour. Other spices or herbs are often added to improve the flavour. These pickled vegetables can be stored for a short period of time (longer if chemically treated for long shelf life).

Fermenting, on the other hand, occurs when microorganisms such as bacteria or fungus transform a food by breaking down sugars and carbohydrates and converting them into acids, carbon dioxide or alcohol. Like pickled foods, fermented foods usually taste sour, but the sourness is produced by the chemical reaction between sugars and microorganisms, not by adding acid.

Some foods are pickled and also fermented. The vegetables start off by being soaked in brine (salty liquid), but are then transformed by lactic acid bacteria, which occurs naturally in vegetables. Kimchi and sauerkraut, which are both made from cabbage and often other vegetables as well, are two examples of foods that start off as pickles but then are sealed in containers to soak for days or weeks as they ferment, to become delicious and long-lasting preserved foods.

Fermented foods are full of nutrients and have many health benefits. They are important in the diets of many different countries.

Find out about these fermented foods and how they are made: **miso**, a fermented soybean paste used as a seasoning; **kefir**, a tangy yogurt-like drink; and **kombucha**, fermented green or black tea.

3   **Find words in the text that match these meanings.**

a   substances that provide nourishment ....

b   a substance that is a made up of two or more ingredients ....

c   tiny living cells that are too small to be seen ....

d   to separate something into smaller parts ....

e   to change something completely ....

4   **Answer these questions using information from the article in Exercise 2.**

a   What are two similarities between pickling and fermenting?

....

....

b   What are two differences between pickling and fermenting?

....

....

5   **Complete this flowchart with information from the text.**

How lactic acid is produced in pickled cabbage

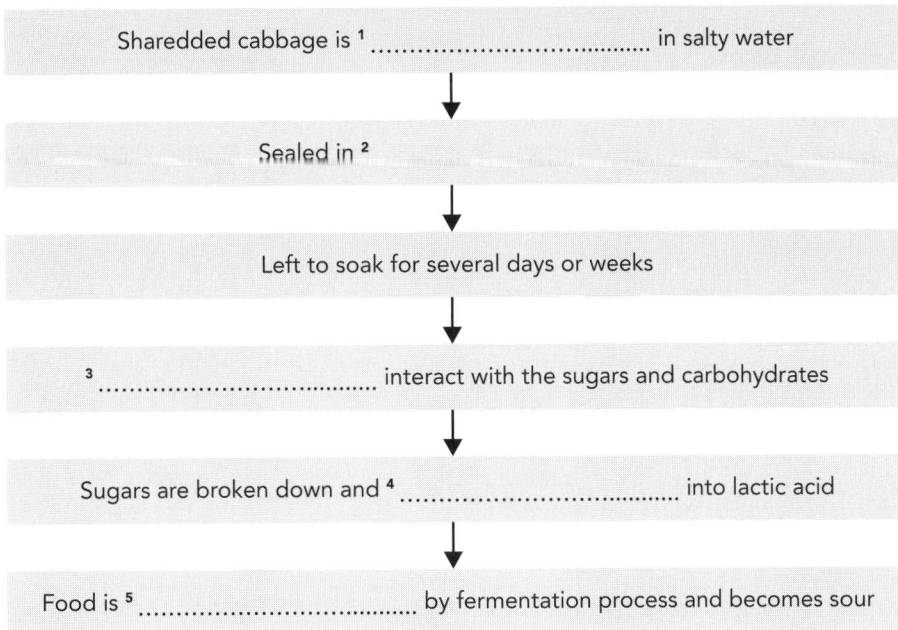

Sharedded cabbage is [1] .... in salty water

↓

Sealed in [2] ....

↓

Left to soak for several days or weeks

↓

[3] .... interact with the sugars and carbohydrates

↓

Sugars are broken down and [4] .... into lactic acid

↓

Food is [5] .... by fermentation process and becomes sour

Challenge

6   **Research one of the fermented foods mentioned in the article and find out how it is made. Create a flowchart in your notebook to show the process. What are its health benefits?**

Use of English: Gerunds and infinitives

This year I've been trying to have a healthier diet. I decided to stop eating meat and eat more vegetables and legumes instead. At first, I started experimenting with new recipes and even persuaded my mum to try making them as well. Then I went on to take a vegetarian cookery class online. It was so much fun! I expected to miss the taste of meat, but in the end, I managed to avoid eating meat products without any difficulty, and I haven't once regretted becoming vegetarian. Of course, my mum always remembers to include a vegetarian option in our family meals, but my friends sometimes forget to tell me that they've chosen a restaurant with very few vegetarian options! That can be a bit awkward.

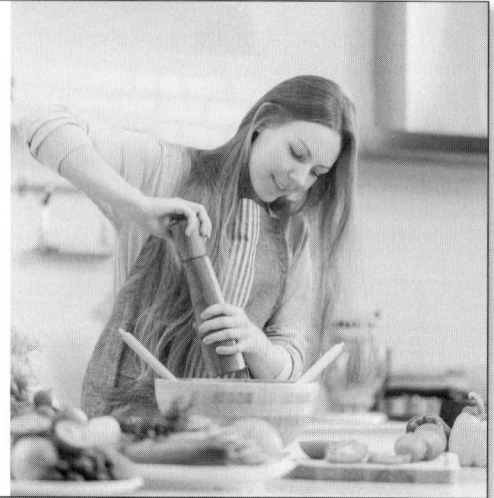

Check!

1   Underline verbs followed by gerunds and infinitives in the text above.

Notice

2   Write the verbs from Exercise 1 below.

    a   Verbs followed by gerunds or infinitives with <u>no</u> change of meaning

       ....

    b   Verbs followed by gerunds or infinitives with a change of meaning

       ....

    c   Verbs only followed by a gerund

       ....

    d   Verbs only followed by an infinitive

       ....

Focus

3   Circle the correct word to complete each sentence. In one sentence, both options are correct.

    a   We tried *to persuade / persuade* Peter to join us for a meal, but he refused.

b   I was really hungry, so I stopped *to eat / eating* a sandwich on my way to school.

c   The lights in the restaurant went out but we all went on *eating / to eat* anyway.

d   I remember *eating / to eat* octopus for the very first time – I thought it was weird!

e   We forgot *bringing / to bring* a packed lunch and ate in a café instead.

f   They wanted to go for a picnic, but it began *to rain / raining* just as they left the house.

Practice

4   **Rewrite these sentences using the verbs provided.**

a   I'm sorry I was late. (apologise)

   ....

b   I hope to see you again on Saturday! (look forward to)

   ....

c   I managed to bake a loaf of bread! (succeed)

   ....

d   The teacher gave us permission for a one-hour lunch break. (allow)

   ....

e   They told us that trying that new restaurant was a great idea! (encourage)

   ....

Challenge

5   **Complete the text using the gerund or infinitive form of the verbs provided.**

My parents were always keen on ....[1] (cook) healthy food. They encouraged us ....[2] (eat) lots of vegetables and fruit every day. They didn't prevent us from ....[3] (buy) occasional snacks and didn't mind us ....[4] (have) crisps or chocolate occasionally, but usually they persuaded us ....[5] (choose) an apple or a banana instead. I started ....[6] (help) with meals when I was eight or nine. At first, I just managed ....[7] (chop) vegetables and salads, but when I got used to ....[8] (do) that, I began ....[9] (invent) my own recipes, and some of them were quite good! I'm looking forward to ....[10] (start) a course in food and nutrition at school next year.

> ### GET IT RIGHT!
>
> Some verbs have an object that is followed by an infinitive. These verbs include *encourage, persuade, advise, allow.*
>
> Example:
> *They encouraged **me to try** a healthier diet.* (not *trying*)
>
> Other verbs are followed by a preposition that is then followed by a gerund or a noun. These verbs include *succeed in, apologise for, look forward to, get used to.*
>
> Example:
> *I look forward **to hearing** your reply.* (not *to hear*)

Use of English: Conditional structures

USE OF ENGLISH

What do you think about school vending machines that sell snacks and sugary drinks?

☐ If teenagers reduce their sugar intake, they will be able to concentrate better.

☐ Occasional sugary snacks and drinks are fine, as long as you don't overdo it.

☐ Provided that you have a healthy diet, some crisps now and again won't do any harm.

☐ If snack bars had been banned from schools, children would have grown up with healthier eating habits.

☐ Teenagers wouldn't learn how to make healthy food choices if a variety of food wasn't available.

☐ Snack bars are OK, on condition that they aren't labelled 'healthy' or 'nutritious'.

Check!

1   Read the opinions above about snacks and drinks in schools.
    Underline the verbs in each sentence. Which opinions do you agree with?

Notice

2   Read the opinions above again. Which ones have the following patterns of tenses?
    Write a–d next to each sentence. (Remember that the order of tenses can be reversed.)

    a   present tense + present tense   c   simple past + *would* verb
    b   present tense + will verb   d   past perfect + would have verb

3   Match the patterns of tenses in Exercise 2 with the descriptions below.

    i   a past situation that cannot be changed ....

    ii   an imaginary situation that is unlikely ....

    iii something that is generally true ....

    iv   something that is a realistic possibility ....

4   Which phrases in Exercise 1 can be replaced by *if*?

    ....

Focus

5   Match each sentence or question from a–f with i–vi.

a   If people didn't eat meat

b   Eating a plant-based diet is healthy

c   It's easy to cut down on salt and sugar

d   If sugary foods were more expensive

e   I could have prevented high blood pressure

f   If you eat more vegetables and fruit

i   as long as you make sure all essential nutrients are included.

ii   how would they get their protein?

iii   if I had reduced my salt intake.

iv   people wouldn't buy them.

v   provided that you read the nutrition labels carefully.

vi   you won't feel hungry for sugary snacks.

Practice

**6   Combine the words to make conditional sentences.
Add or change the form of words as necessary.**

a   I / buy soft drinks / be low in calories / provided that

   ....

b   you / eat more for lunch / not have so many snacks yesterday / if

   ....

c   I go on a vegan diet / be able to find non-dairy cheese / on the condition that

   ....

d   you / not drink so much coffee / sleep better / if

   ....

e   I / not mind eating meat / be well-cooked / as long as

   ....

> **GET IT RIGHT!**
>
> Remember that *will*, *would* or *would have* are only used in the main clause of a conditional sentence, not in the *if* clause.
>
> Examples:
> *If I cooked all my own food, I **would** save money.* (not *if I would cook*)
>
> ***You'll** have more energy if you eat a banana for breakfast.* (not *if you will eat*)

Challenge

7   What are your opinions about eating the following foods? Write three sentences using *as long as*, *provided that* and *on condition that* in your notebook.

eggs   meat   fish   chocolate   crisps

I wouldn't mind eating eggs if chickens were kept in ....

cage-free farms. ....

....

....

....

Academic writing: An opinion essay

1 **Look at the photo. Answer the questions.**

a Why do people like to eat sugary snacks and drinks?

....

b What do you think is the best way to discourage people from buying too many of them? Write one suggestion.

....

2 **Which of the following are true for an opinion essay? Tick the correct answers. Two sentences are incorrect.**

- [ ] Copy language from the essay title.
- [ ] State your opinion clearly at the beginning.
- [ ] Support your opinion with examples.
- [ ] Consider the opposing point of view.
- [ ] Make general statements that are difficult to prove.
- [ ] Restate your opinion in the conclusion.

3 **Read the essay question. Then complete the graphic organiser with your ideas about the topic. Consider the questions in the box to help you.**

Having an extra tax on foods and drinks that contain a lot of sugar will discourage people from buying sugary products, and their diet will be healthier as a result. To what extent do you agree or disagree with this view?

> **WRITING TIP**
>
> In an opinion essay, you may consider opposing arguments, but state why you consider them to be invalid or insignificant.

What categories of food should be taxed?

Will people really buy healthier food instead?

Should companies make their products healthier?

Would clearer labelling work just as well?

Should the government interfere with people's food choices?

Agree		Disagree
....	Tax on sugary foods	....

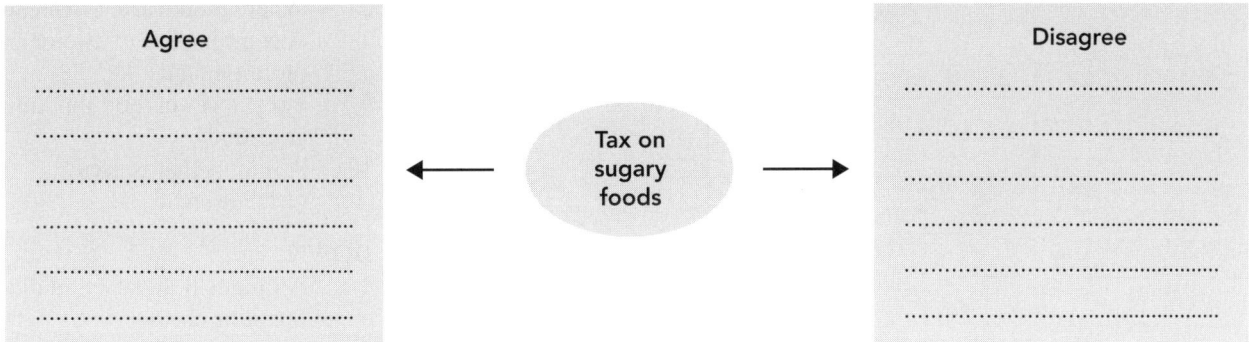

4   Read these sentences from two different essay conclusions.
    Which sentences agree with the sugar tax and which disagree?
    Then put the conclusions into the correct order by writing a number in each box.

☐   a   A better option would be to label unhealthy food more clearly as causing heart disease and obesity.

☐   b   Furthermore, companies may decide to absorb the cost of the tax in order to maintain their sales.

☐   c   If sugary snacks and drinks are more expensive, people will not be able to afford them and will reduce their intake.

☐   d   In conclusion, it is my view that a tax on sugary foods and drinks may help to change eating habits.

☐   e   In my opinion, it would be a good idea to introduce such a tax alongside other measures such as clearer labelling and better health education.

☐   f   Moreover, revenue from this sugar tax could be used to promote health and nutrition programmes.

☐   g   People who love sugary snacks and drinks will find it difficult to give them up and will spend less money on other things in order to buy them.

☐   h   To sum up, it is my opinion that a sugar tax will not have a significant impact on eating habits.

Agree: ....

Disagree: ....

5   Write an essay answering the question in Exercise 3 in your notebook.
    Use your notes from the graphic organiser to help you.

Check your progress

Vocabulary

1 Use the clues to complete the crossword with words from this unit.

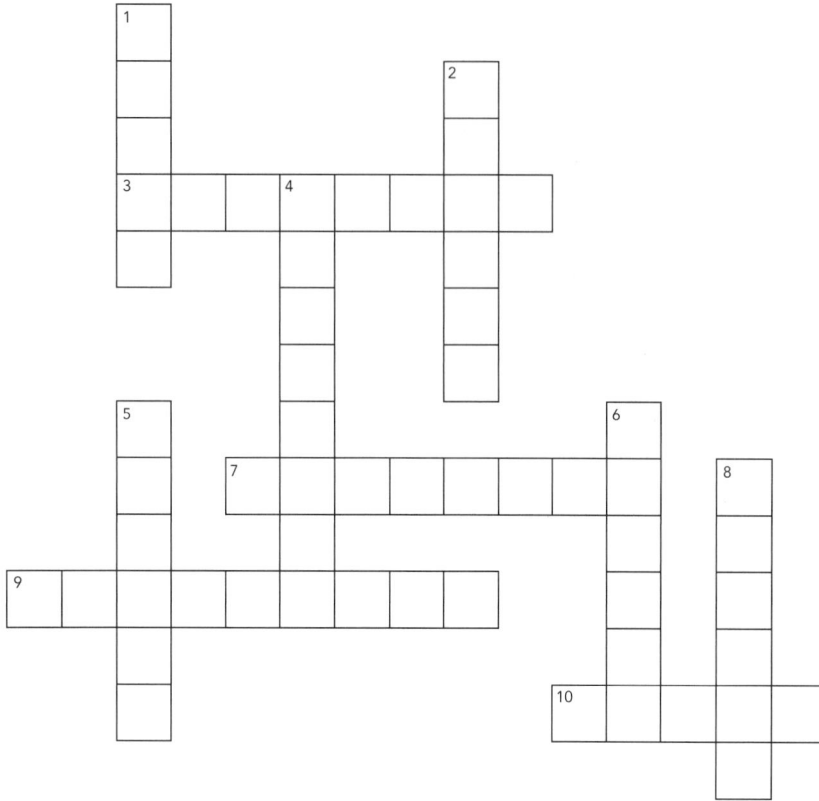

ACROSS
3 Where food waste often ends up
7 A combination of two or more elements
9 Substances in food that nourish your body
10 A fungus that is used to ferment bread

DOWN
1 A fungus that grows on old bread or cheese
2 Peas and lentils are examples of these
4 To identify a disease from symptoms
5 A substance that is found in grains such as wheat
6 Describes something that can be eaten
8 A type of dairy food

Grammar

2 Circle the correct words to complete each sentence.

a We agreed *to go / going* to an Italian restaurant for my birthday.

b My teacher encouraged me *to enter / entering* the cooking competition.

c I couldn't avoid *to eat / eating* crisps when I went to the party.

d If I *had eaten / ate* lunch earlier, I wouldn't have been late for the meeting.

e I'll cook dinner as long as you *wash / will wash* the dishes.

f I wouldn't eat fast food if I *had / have* more time to cook at home.

Reading

3 Look at the photo and read the title of the article. Before reading, answer these questions. After reading, check your answers.

a Which countries produce the most tea?

....

b What happens to the leaves after they are picked?

....

c Why are there different colours of tea?

....

How tea is made

Tea is grown in many countries around the world, the biggest producers being China and India. After the tea leaves are harvested, they are taken to a factory for processing. First, the leaves are laid out on a wire mesh to be dried. This process is known as withering and takes 12–18 hours. Then the leaves are rolled in a machine that twists and turns them so that they dry out and start to release enzymes. The next stage of the process is oxidisation, sometimes known as fermentation. The leaves are laid out on a table for up to two hours in a warm, moist environment. During this time, enzymes inside the leaves react with the oxygen in the air and the leaves change colour from green to brown. The degree of oxidisation determines the taste and strength of the tea. Some black teas are fermented for years, whereas green teas are not fermented at all. Once they have reached the correct level of oxidisation, they go through hot air dryers to stop oxidisation and remove any remaining moisture.

4   Complete the flowchart with words from the text. Write one word in each box.

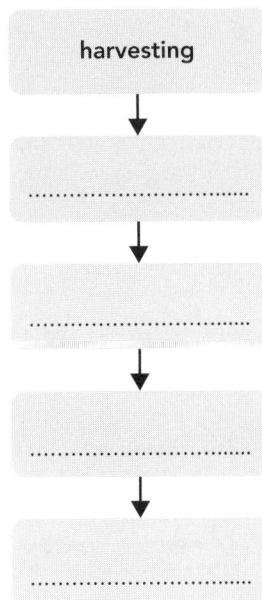

```
   harvesting
       ↓
  .................
       ↓
  .................
       ↓
  .................
       ↓
  .................
```

Writing

5   Read the essay question and make notes for and against for your response. Then decide whether you agree or disagree with the statement. Write the essay in your notebook.

Many people regularly eat fast food, which can lead to heart disease and obesity. Some have suggested that a complete ban on fast food would help us all to be healthier. To what extent do you agree or disagree?

REFLECTION

Write answers to these questions in your notebook.

a   How do you interpret the unit title after studying this unit?

b   Name three important decisions you have made about your food choices recently.

c   List four ways you might change your diet in the future. Use the verbs *stop*, *start*, *decide* and *avoid* with conditional structures.

d   What do you think are the most important issues concerning food in the world today?

e   What advice would you give yourself to improve your writing of an opinion essay?

4 The well-being of sport

Think about it: Sport for all

1   Read the responses about sport below.
    Match the words in the box with the responses.

> attention span   determination   joy   mindful   self-confidence
> self-control   self-esteem   sense of belonging   well-being

Why do you like sport? We asked you and here's what you said.

a
I love playing football. I go to the park every Saturday to practise with my friends. Why? Because it's fun!

....

b
I play volleyball. It's an exciting sport and I enjoy being part of a team. We get along together really well. I think we respect each other and our coach too, of course!

....

c
I've been doing gymnastics since I was five and it's really competitive. I have to practise a lot but it's worth it. When I feel I've done the very best I can, I feel proud of my achievement!

....

d
I go running every day before school. I think it's good for my health. If I'm fit and keep active, I generally feel good physically, and mentally as well.

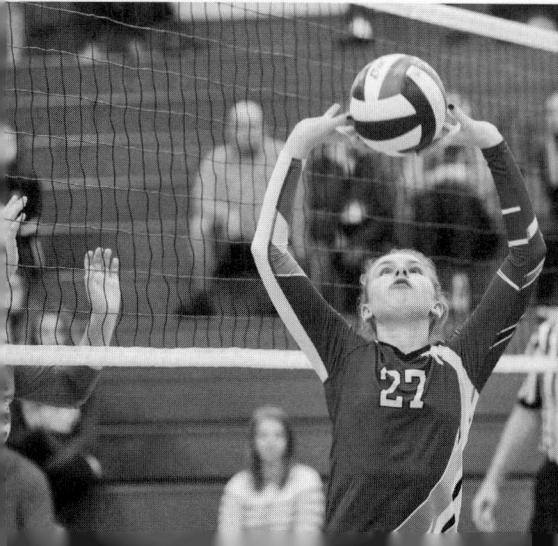

....

e I think it's a good preparation for life really, because in real life you have to cope with ups and downs, and you need to keep trying if you want to win.

....

f I like track and field and I think it helps me to concentrate. When you're practising, you have to stay really focused. I think it helps me with my schoolwork too.

....

g Our coach teaches us to use special techniques to stay calm before a match, like using visualisation and things like that. It helps to focus on the present moment. I think it really works!

....

h I think it's good for me because I can run around and let off steam. It helps me manage my emotions better in other situations later.

....

2   Read this part of a lecture about the benefits of doing sport.
Complete the script with signpost phrases from the box.

Another way that	Let's start by	Let's turn to
One reason may be	To explain more about that	

....¹ looking at how sports activities can help

improve cognitive skills. We all know that doing sports has physical benefits. But

being active also has cognitive benefits. ....²,

let's look at this graph from a research study that shows improved

academic performance in students that did sports. Why does this happen?

....³ the increased blood flow to the brain.

....⁴ physical activity impacts your mental state

is by activating endorphins. Endorphins can improve your mood, making you

more willing to attempt ambitious goals. ....⁵

other benefits of doing sport and look at how it affects social and

communications skills…

Challenge

3   Interview three of your classmates. Find out what sports they like and what they
think are the benefits of doing sports. Write a summary in your notebook.

Psychology and physical education: Mental health in elite sport

1   Read the article below.
    Underline the parts that are relevant to writing a summary of Francisca's life.

Paralympic sports hero and role model – Francisca Mardones

At 43 years old, Francisca Mardones represented her country of Chile at the 2020 Paralympic Games in Tokyo. Taking part in the Paralympics had been a dream of hers and she has represented her country three times. She previously competed as a wheelchair tennis player in the 2012 and 2016 Summer Paralympics, but after a hand injury she decided to switch to athletics, focusing on **shot put**, **discus throwing** and **javelin**. In 2020, she became the first female Chilean Paralympic athlete to get a gold medal, competing in shot put. She set a world record with an 8.33 m shot.

Francisca first took up wheelchair tennis after she was injured in 1999 during a hurricane in Puerto Rico, where she was working as a hotel manager. As the massive storm swept across the country, Francisca was caught outside, thrown over a cliff and her back was broken. She managed to drag herself to safety and remained there alone for two days, cold and in agonising pain, waiting to be rescued.

After a year in hospital and 20 back operations, she had to face the fact that she would no longer be able to move her legs. But she didn't give up. 'Your life will change only if you want to,' she said. At first, wheelchair tennis was part of her path to recovery, but it soon became an inspiration to achieve much more. 'I have always put all my energy into everything I do. It is very satisfying to see that you are capable of surpassing yourself, of breaking all your barriers,' she said.

In addition to her world records, medals and numerous awards, Francisca is also an accomplished motivational speaker. Her inspiring story of overcoming adversity to achieve success makes her a role model for future athletes. She gives talks on topics such as teamwork, motivation, self-care, prevention of risks, and resilience. 'Motivating children to be our future champions is what fills my heart the most! No matter how old you are, don't stop believing in yourself because you can be whatever you want to be!' she said.

shot put: throwing a heavy metal ball from your shoulder

discus throwing: throwing a circular flat metal plate

javelin: throwing a long stick with a pointed end

2   Answer the questions in your own words.

a   What do you find most amazing about Francisca's story?

....

b   How do you think sport has helped Francisca's physical and mental well-being?

....

c   How would you describe Francisca's personal qualities?

....

d   What obstacles do you think Francisca might have faced in her athletic career?

....

e   What do you think Francisca talks about in her talk on the topic of 'self-care'?

....

3   Find these words in the passage.
Then match the words with their meanings from the box.

obstacles   inspiring   do better   ability to recover

a   adversity   obstacles

b   resilience   ....

c   surpass   ....

d   motivating   ....

Challenge

4   Read the article about Francisca Mardones again. Imagine that you are a sports
journalist. Write a list of questions you would like to ask Francisca.
Use the words in the box.

anxiety   elite sports   pressure   sporting discipline   support

....

....

....

....

....

....

READING TIP

When you read an article, it is sometimes helpful to look at the text from different points of view. What would the following people find most interesting in this article?

- a sports coach
- a child who wants to become an athlete
- an athlete who wants to improve their performance
- a documentary film maker

Use of English: The passive

Olympic sports

How are new sports selected for the Olympics? Four new sports were added to the Olympics for the Tokyo 2020 Games: karate, skateboarding, sport climbing and surfing. For the Paris Olympics in 2024, skateboarding, sport climbing, breakdancing and surfing were chosen. Some sports, like baseball, have been included, but later got left out. And some sports like cricket and squash have never been approved. It's easier for a sport to be accepted if it is popular around the world, especially with young people, and if expensive facilities are not required. What new sports will be selected for the next Olympic Games? Netball, bowling, dancing and parkour are just some of the sports that are being considered.

Check!

1   Underline the uses of the passive in the text above. Then match them with the categories below.

    a   present simple passive   ....

    b   present continuous passive   ....

    c   past simple passive   ....

    d   present perfect passive   ....

    e   future passive   ....

    f   passive infinitive form   ....

Notice

2   Which examples do the following?

    a   Use more than one auxiliary   ....

    b   Use irregular past participles   ....

    c   Use a modal verb   ....

    d   Describe a negative event   ....

Focus

3 Circle the correct words to complete these sentences.

a Sports such as football are often *sponsor* / *(sponsored)* by large companies.

b Athletes with disabilities have *given* / *been given* better access to training and facilities.

c Sports matches are *monitor* / *monitored* by video cameras to avoid disputes.

d Sports stadiums will *develop* / *be developed* more sustainable models.

e How will the popularity of Esports *impact* / *be impacted* on traditional sports?

Practice

4 Correct the mistake in each sentence.

a We were ~~inviting~~ invited to play tennis with them next month.

b The coach fired from his job after they lost too many matches.

c Snowboarding was introducing as an Olympic sport in 1998.

d The club been given a donation by a big tech company.

e The players will be inform about the match dates next week.

Challenge

5 Read the email and complete the text using the passive or active form of verbs in the box.

| not broadcast | expect | explain | give | invite |
| organise | not pay | select | visit | win |

Hi Ella!

You'll never guess what we did last weekend! We visited .¹ the football club and ....² a tour of the stadium and clubhouse! The event ....³ by our sports teacher. He knows we're all football fans! It was so cool to see all the training rooms and the club facilities. They have a special room for all the medals and cups that ....⁴. The guide ....⁵ the history of the club. Football was really different in the old days. Footballers ....⁶ that much and matches ....⁷ on TV, only on radio. Nowadays, footballers ....⁸ to give interviews all the time and post messages on social media. At the end of the tour, we ....⁹ to sign up for the youth coaching team. I'm so excited – maybe I ....¹⁰ for the school football team next year!

Let's meet up soon!

Jonas

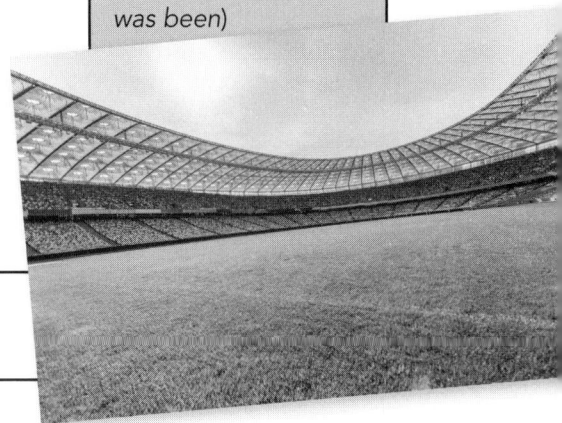

Use of English: Comparative and superlative forms

USE OF ENGLISH

The Most Popular Sports in the World

What are the most popular sports in the world? Football has the highest number of fans at around 4 billion, a much higher number than cricket, which only has 2.5 billion fans. Tennis is more popular than volleyball, with volleyball having 100 million fewer fans. Rugby is less popular than baseball, which has 25 million more fans. The least popular sport is golf. It has the lowest number of fans at 450 million.

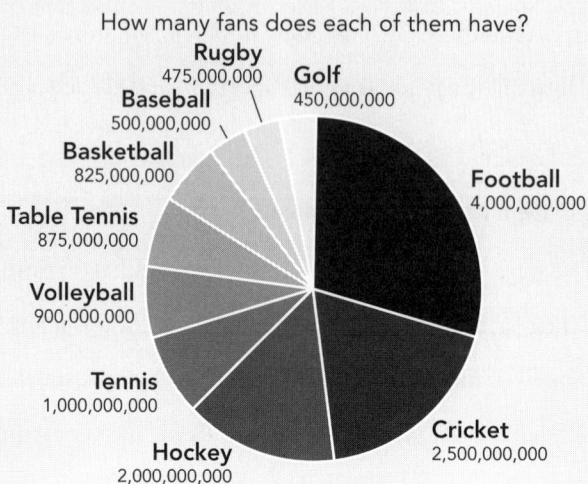

How many fans does each of them have?

Rugby 475,000,000
Golf 450,000,000
Baseball 500,000,000
Basketball 825,000,000
Table Tennis 875,000,000
Volleyball 900,000,000
Tennis 1,000,000,000
Hockey 2,000,000,000
Football 4,000,000,000
Cricket 2,500,000,000

Check!

1   Read the information above and underline all the examples of comparative and superlative forms.

Notice

2   Which examples use the following?

    a   the *-er* or *-est* form of an adjective   ....

    b   *more or less* with an adjective   ....

    c   *more* or *less* with a noun   ....

    d   *fewer* or *fewest* with a countable noun   ....

Focus

3   **Study the chart again. Complete each sentence with a word from the options given.**

		far	very	quite
a	Football is .far. more popular than any other sport.	far	very	quite
b	Table tennis is .... as popular as volleyball.	much	almost	more
c	Tennis has 1 million .... fans than hockey.	less	fewer	more
d	The sport that has the .... fans is golf.	less	least	fewest

e   Basketball is not .... as popular as table tennis.   almost   so   quite

f   Rugby is .... popular than baseball.   many   less   more

Practice

4   **Rewrite each sentence using *much* or *more* and a comparative.**

a   Hockey is extremely fast. Volleyball is quite fast.

   Hockey is much faster than volleyball. ....

b   Football is popular in lots of countries. Rugby is popular in a few countries.

   ....

c   Golf players earn a lot of money. Volleyball players don't earn as much.

   ....

d   Cricket matches take a very long time. Football matches are shorter.

   ....

e   There weren't a lot of winter snow sports in the past. Now there are dozens.

   ....

Challenge

5   **Complete the text with words from the box.**

healthiest   best   fewer   much   healthier   less   more   older   most

What do you think is the .....healthiest.....¹ sport? Some people think swimming

is the ....² sport for overall muscle strength and fitness. Swimmers

report that they feel ....³ less stress after swimming and there are

also ....⁴ possibilities for injury than in some other sports. Others

claim that sports such as basketball and volleyball are ....⁵ as they

require ....⁶ agility and spatial coordination. Runners will tell you

that running has the ....⁷ health benefits. Unlike swimming and

ball sports, you don't need any special equipment or facilities (apart from running

shoes) and runners are ....⁸ likely to experience bone and muscle

loss as they get ....⁹.

6   **Compare two sports, saying which one is healthier and why.**
   Write a paragraph in your notebook.

GET IT RIGHT!

Remember that when we use an adjective with *-er*, we do not need the word *more*. If we want to make the comparative adjective stronger, we can use *much* or *far*. When using *more* with a noun, we use *much* with uncountable nouns or *many* with countable nouns to make it stronger.

Examples:
*Basketball is **much easier** to play than hockey.* (not *more easier*)

*Football has **many more** women players now than in the past.* (not *much more*)

*You need **much more** sport equipment to play golf than to play football.* (not *many more*)

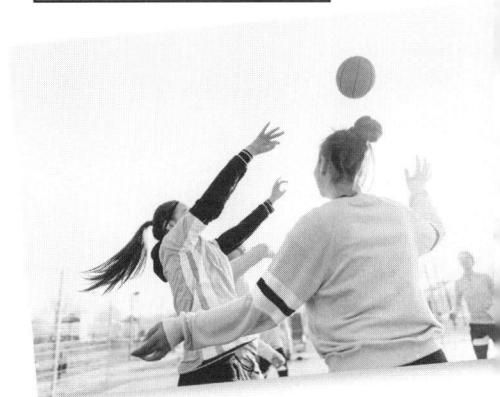

Academic writing: Describing data in graphs and charts

1   **Look at the chart and use the information to complete the text.**

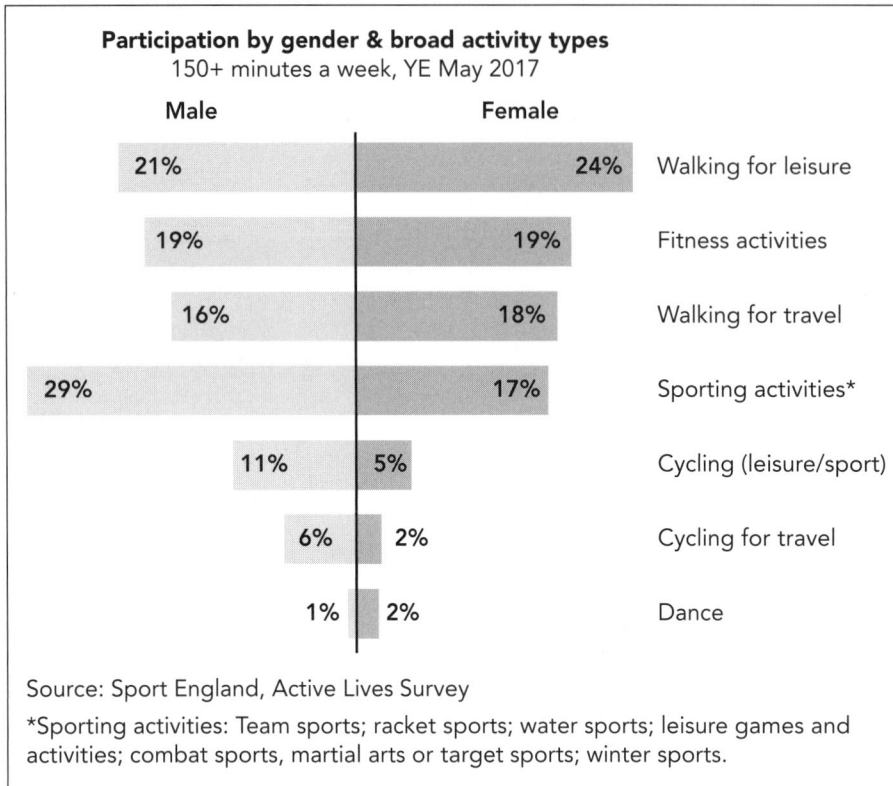

Participation by gender & broad activity types
150+ minutes a week, YE May 2017

Male	Female	
21%	24%	Walking for leisure
19%	19%	Fitness activities
16%	18%	Walking for travel
29%	17%	Sporting activities*
11%	5%	Cycling (leisure/sport)
6%	2%	Cycling for travel
1%	2%	Dance

Source: Sport England, Active Lives Survey

*Sporting activities: Team sports; racket sports; water sports; leisure games and activities; combat sports, martial arts or target sports; winter sports.

WRITING TIP

When you describe a chart, it's a good idea to start by giving an overview of the information. You can describe the topic and say what each part of the chart represents. After that, you could select the most important details and make comparisons where relevant. Try to use linking words to connect your ideas.

The chart gives information about *which sports activities are popular with adults* ....[1] in England. The bars on the left-hand side show ....[2]. Those on the right-hand side show ....[3]. The length of each bar corresponds with ....[4]. The chart shows that the most popular activities for men are ....[5] and for women ....[6]. The least popular activity for both men and women is ....[7] and for women it is also ....[8]. The activity that showed the greatest difference between men and women is ....[9], while the activity that was equally popular with both men and women was ....[10] ....[11] and ....[12] were slightly less popular with men than with women, whereas ....[13] were significantly less popular with women than with men.

2   Study the chart. Answer the questions.

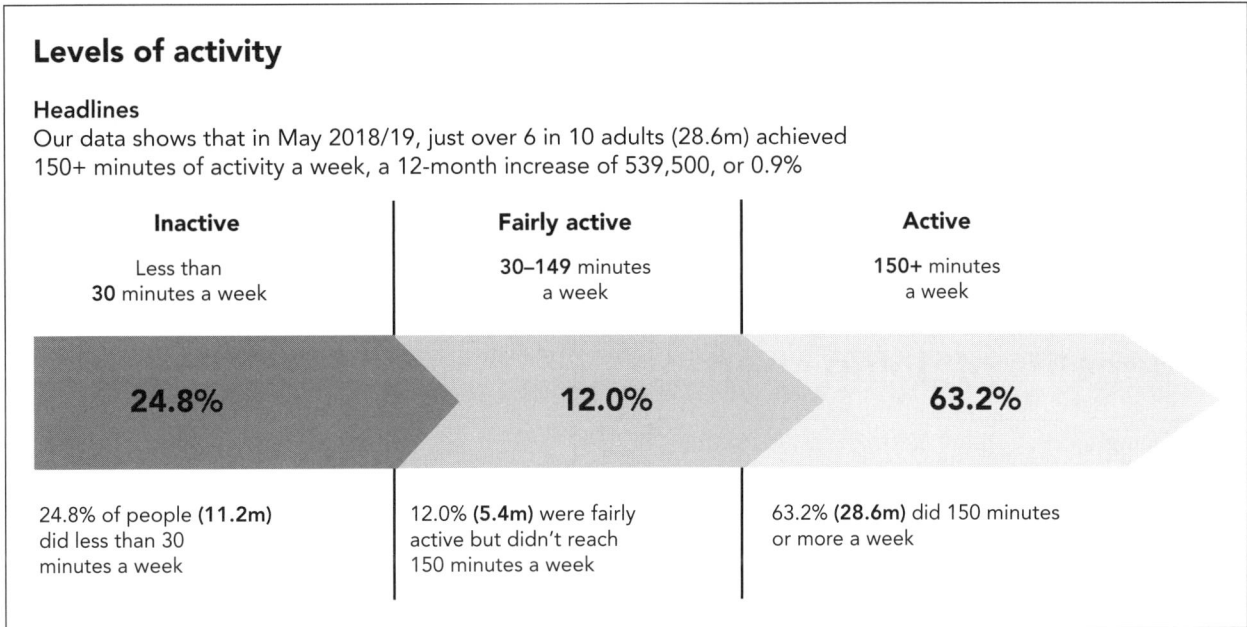

Levels of activity

Headlines
Our data shows that in May 2018/19, just over 6 in 10 adults (28.6m) achieved
150+ minutes of activity a week, a 12-month increase of 539,500, or 0.9%

Inactive	Fairly active	Active
Less than 30 minutes a week	30–149 minutes a week	150+ minutes a week
24.8%	**12.0%**	**63.2%**
24.8% of people **(11.2m)** did less than 30 minutes a week	12.0% **(5.4m)** were fairly active but didn't reach 150 minutes a week	63.2% **(28.6m)** did 150 minutes or more a week

a   What is the main topic of the graphic?

   ....

b   What categories does it compare?

   ....

c   Which category has the greatest and least percentage of people?

   ....

d   Approximately what proportion of the population is in each category?

   ....

e   What reason do you think people might have for not being active?

   ....

f   What effects do you think there might be of being inactive?

   ....

**3   Use your answers to write a summary of the chart in your notebook.
Use the summary in Exercise 1 as a model.**

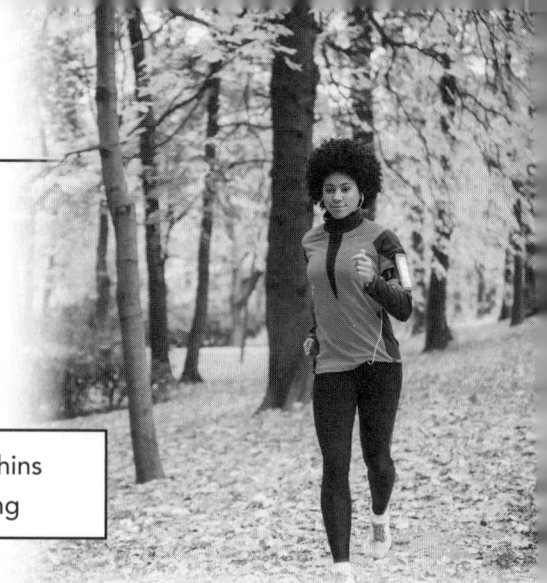

Check your progress

Vocabulary

1   Complete the text with words from the box.

anxiety belonging depression determination endorphins physical pressure self-confidence support well-being

Benefits of doing sport

Doing sport at school has many health benefits, both ....physical....... [1] and mental. When you are physically active, the brain releases ....[2], which boost your mood and contribute to your overall sense of ....[3]. Secondly, as you become more successful in your sport, you start to believe in yourself and you gain ....[4]. You become more resilient and are able to face failure with renewed ....[5] to succeed. There are social benefits too. Being part of team brings a sense of ....[6] and you can rely on your team mates for ....[7]. Physical activity has been shown to have a positive impact on mental health, helping to prevent negative thoughts that can lead to ....[8] and ....[9], and helping to deal with emotional and psychological ....[10].

Grammar

2   Rewrite these sentences so that they have the same meaning. Use the words provided.

a   The coach has given us some instructions.

We ....

....

b   They dropped several sports from the last Olympics.

Several sports ....

....

c   Will they show the match on TV?

Will the match ....

....?

d   90% of students are physically active every day. Ten years ago, it was only 60%.

In the past, ...

....

e   Most students in our school play football. (popular)

....

....

f   85% of students do team sports, 12% do individual sports. (more)

....

....

Reading

3 Skim the paragraph and circle the best title.

A Reasons why young people want to become athletes

B Why young athletes should think about mental health

C How to get started in a career as an athlete

> Athletes who compete at the highest level of their sport often start their sporting career at a young age. It takes an enormous amount of time and commitment, not only from the players themselves, but also from their family, teachers and their coaches. Given such a huge investment of time and money, young athletes face enormous pressure to succeed. As a result, they may push themselves too hard, which can cause physical injury or mental exhaustion. That's why it is so important for young athletes to be proactive about mental health and develop strategies for reducing stress and avoiding burnout.

4 Find five words or phrases in the text in Exercise 3 that describe negative effects of competition on young athletes and underline them.

5 Suggest three ways to avoid some of these negative effects. Write them in your notebook.

Writing

6 Study the charts. Write a summary in your notebook.

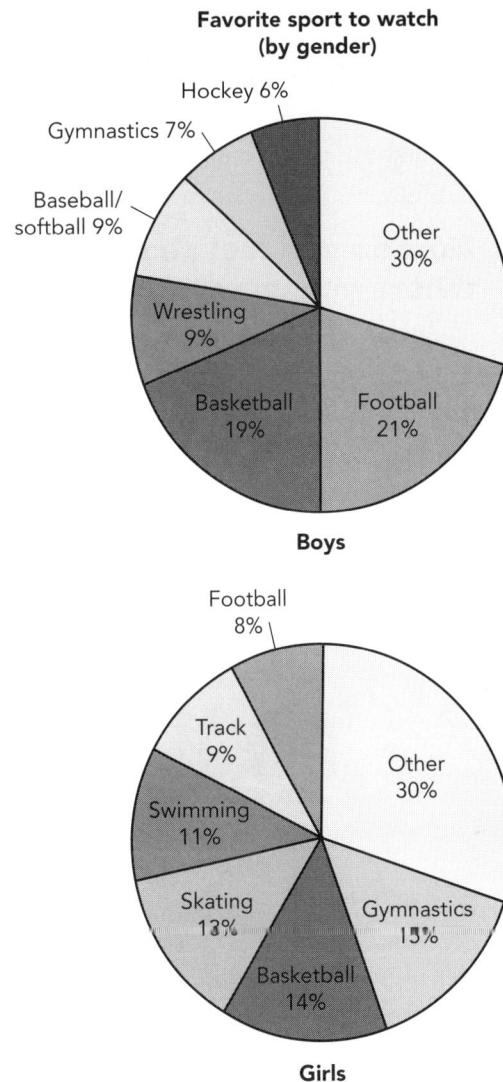

Favorite sport to watch (by gender)

Hockey 6%
Gymnastics 7%
Baseball/softball 9%
Wrestling 9%
Basketball 19%
Football 21%
Other 30%

Boys

Football 8%
Track 9%
Swimming 11%
Skating 13%
Basketball 14%
Gymnastics 15%
Other 30%

Girls

REFLECTION

Write answers to these questions in your notebook.

a What new information did you learn about sports from doing this unit?

b How important are sports in your life? Explain why.

c Read one of your writing tasks from this unit and find three places to introduce passive structures into your writing.

d What are the most popular sports in your country? Write three sentences about them using comparatives and superlatives.

e What did you improve in your listening and speaking skills in this unit? What did you do well?

5 Changing places

Think about it: Third culture kids

1   Read the descriptions and answer the questions that follow.

> ### How do you feel about living in a culture that is different from where you were born or grew up?
>
> **Dev**
>
> We moved from country to country when I was a child because of my father's job. It was difficult starting a new school every year. Even though I went to international schools where English was spoken, somehow I was never able to fit in and make friends. Even now I don't feel at home anywhere and have found it difficult to **put down roots**.
>
> **Sonia**
>
> I was born in Argentina. We lived there until I was ten and then we moved to the UK. I was totally **uprooted!** I felt so **homesick.** It was really hard trying to adapt without losing my **cultural roots**. I still identify more with my birth culture, even though I have lived in the UK for 20 years now.
>
> **Junko**
>
> I was born in Brazil but my parents both came from Japan and we spoke Japanese at home. When I was 20, I decided to try living in Japan for a year and got a job there. But it was much more difficult than I thought. Even though I looked Japanese and spoke the language fluently, I still felt like a foreigner and even had a sort of **identity crisis** while I was there.
>
> **Pete**
>
> I was born in Australia but we went to live in Indonesia when I was three because my parents had jobs at a university there. We lived there for five years before coming back to Australia. We live in Perth, but it took a while for me to **settle down** when we came back. I think that wherever you spend your **formative years** has a big influence on your **cultural identity**, no matter where you were born.

Match the descriptions to the correct person.

a   Felt very homesick   ....

b   Lives in the country where they were born   ....

c   Thinks that where you were born is the biggest influence   ....

d   Had difficulty making friends   ....

e   Tried to adapt to a new culture but couldn't   ....

f   Thinks that were you grew up is the biggest influence   ....

g   Tried to discover their cultural roots   ....

2   **Match the words in bold in the people's descriptions in Exercise 1 with the meanings below.**

a   Early stages of childhood   ....

b   Feel a sense of belonging   ....

c   Feel at home   ....

d   Feel lost   ....

e   Heritage or traditions   ....

f   Miss my home   ....

g   Not sure which culture I belong to   ....

h   Understanding who I am   ....

Challenge

3   **Which of these opinions do you agree or disagree with?**
    Write a few sentences explaining why.

a   I think you should hold on to your culture and traditions wherever you live.
    It's important not to forget your cultural roots.

b   It's important to respect the customs of whichever country you live in and
    behave accordingly.

c   It's a good thing to have cultural diversity in any culture because that enables
    people to understand different views and live in harmony.

d   I think the main thing is to have an open mind and acknowledge that despite
    cultural differences we are all basically the same.

....

....

....

Economics and geography: Megacities

1 **Look at the photo. Answer the questions.**

What do you think are the problems of living in a very large city?
What are the advantages? List five points for and against in your notebook.

2 **Read the article. Underline the advantages and disadvantages of living in a big city.**

Evolution of the megacity

In 1950, there were just two: New York and Tokyo. By 2018, there were 33 cities with more than 10 million people, located on almost every continent around the world, from Sao Paulo to Lagos to Shanghai. It is estimated that by 2030, there will be 41 megacities, many of them in Asia and Africa.

The increase in urbanisation is driven mainly by economics. In the 18th century, as Europe and North America started to industrialise, people moved away from small agricultural communities to find better paid work and more job opportunities in the labour force of the big cities. As well as these kinds of 'pull' factors, there are also 'push' factors. Sometimes harsh conditions force people to move away from rural areas. Conflict, famine, drought, flooding and lack of employment opportunities were some of the reasons people in Ethiopia, Bangladesh, and Darfur in Sudan left their communities and moved to the large cities.

While many megacities initially evolved due to the exodus from rural to city areas, megacities are likely to increase in size due to other factors as well. First,

the population may expand due to natural increase as the number of births exceeds the replacement level. A second reason is that nearby municipalities may also grow and join up with the megacity to form one large conurbation area, known as urban sprawl.

If a city grows too quickly, the infrastructure of the city may not be able to keep pace. Housing, water supplies, electricity lines, sewage and sanitation systems, schools, clinics, roads and public transportation all need to be planned and built for the growing population. Without this infrastructure, people have to live in shanty towns or slums where conditions are unhealthy and diseases can spread more rapidly.

According to the latest report published by UN-Habitat, the UN agency working on urban issues, cities generate economic value when they function efficiently, and are sustainable and resilient. The report calls for urban policies that regulate land use, plan for urban growth, limit urban sprawl and relieve overcrowded housing.

3 The list below gives some reasons for moving to a big city.
Which TWO reasons are mentioned in the text in Exercise 2?

A There is better housing and transportation.

B It is possible to earn more money from your job.

C Cities are expanding and their populations are growing.

D Getting job training and qualifications is easier.

E Cities offer many opportunities to meet people.

F It is less isolated than living in a rural area.

4 The list below gives some disadvantages of living in a big city.
Which TWO reasons are mentioned in the text in Exercise 2?

A There is too much pollution.

B The cost of living is more expensive.

C People spend too much time in traffic jams.

D There is a greater risk of illness.

E There is more crime and violence.

F Housing is insufficient and inadequate.

5 Write definitions for each word or phrase.

a urbanisation: ....

b push and pull factors: ....

c conurbation: ....

d urban sprawl: ....

Challenge

6 Think of three ideas that could help urban planners make cities more sustainable and resilient.

....

....

....

....

....

....

Use of English: Impersonal language

USE OF ENGLISH

Report: Making cities more sustainable

Recent urbanisation has resulted in cities that are congested and unmanageable. It is hoped that the recommendations made in this report will help to make cities more sustainable and resilient for the future. Reducing carbon footprint is considered to be a priority. Public transport systems should be improved in order to relieve traffic congestions and reduce commuter time. Pedestrian and car-free zones that encourage people to walk more would help to reduce air pollution. There are several other recommendations in this report which…

Check!

1   Impersonal language is often used in academic reports to make them sound more objective. Read the text and underline any impersonal language.

Notice

2   Which parts of the report extract above use the following?

   a   A passive verb ....

   b   *It is* as the subject ....

   c   *There are* as the subject ....

   d   A complex noun as the subject ....

Focus

3   Rewrite these sentences using one of the methods described in Exercise 2.

   a   They should ban lorries and trucks from city centres.

   Lorries and trucks ....

   b   If they had more green spaces in cities, people would walk more.

   If there ....

   c   It would reduce overcrowding if there were more regulation of land use.

   Overcrowding ....

   d   We suggest that more affordable housing will improve public health.

   It ....

e   They need to invest more in low-carbon transport.

There ....

Practice

4   Rewrite the sentences using the passive form and the verbs in brackets.

a   Carbon dioxide in the air affects children's mental and physical development. (can)

Children's mental and physical development ....

....

b   Improvements in public transport reduces traffic congestion. (may)

Traffic congestion ....

....

c   Sustainable infrastructure will improve living conditions in big cities. (could)

Living conditions ....

....

d   Creating more bike lanes around the city encourages more people to cycle. (might)

More people ....

....

e   In the future, they won't heat homes with coal or gas. (may)

In the future, homes ....

....

> **LANGUAGE TIP**
>
> In academic writing and reports, it is a good idea to use modal verbs such as *may, might, can* or *could* together with passive structures to qualify or limit statements that are opinions rather than facts.
>
> **Examples:**
> *Many social problems* **can be caused** *by overcrowding.* (not *are caused*)
>
> *Air pollution* **may be reduced** *by creating low-emission zones.* (not *will be reduced*)

Challenge

5   Underline the parts of the paragraph that can be rewritten to use more impersonal language. Then rewrite the paragraph in your notebook.

For this report, we interviewed a group of 20 students about facilities for young people in the city. We covered three main topics: transportation, entertainment and sports facilities. All participants agreed that they don't have enough buses and too much traffic often caused long delays. They felt that the introduction of bus-only lanes would improve the situation. They gave entertainment a top rating as they have just opened a new cinema and concert venue. Concerning sports facilities, everyone knows that the council are planning a new swimming pool, but it would be great to have a new skateboard park as well. We will present the findings to the city council for them to consider at their next urban planning meeting.

Use of English: Reported speech

USE OF ENGLISH

Alicia told us about her new charity fundraising website called Cooking for the World. She told us that she had launched this charity two years ago to collect money for refugees around the world. She said that they had already raised 5000 euros and she was hoping to raise 10,000 more by the end of the year. She explained that anyone could take part by hosting food events in their communities. She told us to visit her website, where she would post news about her next fundraising event.

Check!

1   Read the text and underline the reporting verbs.

2   Write the verb forms that were used in the original conversation.

    a   she had launched   ....

    b   they had already raised   ....

    c   she was hoping   ....

    d   anyone could take part   ....

    e   she would post   ....

Notice

3   Answer these questions about the text.

    a   What are three different ways that the verb *tell* is used?

        ....

    b   What is one important difference between the verb *tell* and the other verbs?

        ....

Focus

4   Complete these sentences using reported speech rules.

    a   Take part in our fundraising effort.

        She told .... take part in .... fundraising effort.

b People from all over the world have been helping us.

They .... people from all over the world ....

c Your money will pay for food, clothing and tents.

He explained .... pay for food, clothing and tents.

d Cooking has helped to bring people together.

She told .... cooking .... to bring people together.

e This is my new international cookbook, *Cooking for the World*.

He told .... new international cookbook, *Cooking for the World*.

Practice

5 **Rewrite the sentences as reported speech.**
Decide if a change of tense is necessary or not.

a 'There aren't enough support services here for refugees,' she complained.

....

b 'I went to a job interview yesterday, but I was turned down,' he revealed.

....

c 'We've raised 10,000 euros in two weeks,' they claimed.

....

d 'Dozens of volunteers were working here, but many have now left,' she explained.

....

e 'It's sometimes difficult to understand them because they speak so quickly,' he admitted.

....

f 'I met several people who worked as interpreters and translators,' he pointed out.

....

GET IT RIGHT!

It is not always necessary to change the tense in reported speech. If the present event is something that is still true, for example, then there is no need to change the tense. This is because the reporter's view of the time of the event and the original speaker's view are the same.

Examples:
*She said that most students at her school **are/were** bilingual.* (As the students are still bilingual now, there is no need to change the tense.)

*He told me that they **had just arrived** the week before.* (As the time of speaking is later than the time of the original statement, a tense shift is needed.)

Challenge

6 **Think of three things your parents or teacher said to you today.**
Write them in your notebook using reported speech.

Academic writing: A report

1   Complete the model report below with phrases from the box.
    Write the correct letter in each gap.
    Then read it again and underline useful phrases.

a	complained that it would	f	The aim of this report
b	it was felt that there were	g	The speaker concluded
c	It was suggested	h	The speaker outlined
d	said that they would	i	The survey included
e	that it would be beneficial	j	This report is based on

Your class recently went to a talk about becoming a volunteer. Your teacher has asked you to write a report about what you learned and give some recommendations for the school committee.

Becoming a volunteer

Introduction

Last week, we attended a talk given by a volunteer from the local community centre.

...........................¹ is to describe what we learned from the talk and suggest ways for students to get more involved with community volunteer work.

...........................² information gathered from a survey completed by 20 students who attended the talk. ....³ questions about personal opinions and recommendations for how to encourage more students to take up volunteer opportunities.

What we learned

...........................⁴ three main ways in which volunteers can take part in volunteer work. First, by fundraising for people who need help. Second, by taking part in programmes that help others, such as the Study Buddy scheme, which partners students with someone of their own age for mentoring. Finally, by spreading information and encouraging others to take part in volunteering. ....⁵ by pointing out that volunteers not only help others, they also learn how to organise, collaborate and become more self-confident. ....⁶ that these skills would also look good on our CV and impress future employers.

Student reactions

Student reactions to the talk were overwhelmingly positive. Eighty percent of students said they felt motivated to take part in volunteer activities. Fifty percent ....[7] actively seek out volunteering opportunities. Only a couple of students ....[8] distract them from their schoolwork. One student said that they had already been a volunteer and had found it to be worthwhile.

Recommendations

Most students agreed ....[9] to have regular updates on volunteering opportunities given out at the school assembly. Several students mentioned setting up a community volunteer club. One person suggested that volunteering should become part of the school curriculum for senior students. In general, ...[10] many reasons why volunteering could benefit both the students and the community.

2   **Read this essay question. Then make notes of your ideas about the topic.**

Your class recently went to a talk about being a global citizen. Your teacher has asked you to write a report about what you learned and make some recommendations for the school committee.

A global citizen is someone who is aware of and understands the wider world and their place in it. They take an active role in their community and work with others to make our planet more peaceful, sustainable and fairer.

Your report should be 300–350 words long.

What is a global citizen? Why is it important?

What can we do to become a global citizen?

What can we change in our school to encourage students to be global citizens?

3   **Use your notes from Exercise 2 to write the report in your notebook.**

Check your progress

Vocabulary

1 Complete these sentences with appropriate words from this unit.

a A .... is a person who has been forced to leave their country because of war or other reasons.

b An .... is someone who comes to a country to live there permanently.

c Your .... are the early stages of childhood up to eight years old.

d Someone can have an .... when they start to question their self or their place in the world.

e If you .... in a place it means that you decide to live there and make your permanent home there.

f If you feel different from everyone around you, it may feel as if you don't ....

Grammar

2 Rewrite the underlined words using impersonal language.

a They have a lot of problems with roads and infrastructure.

b We have implemented new policies to cope with the increased population.

c We advise you to invest in low-carbon transport.

d No one told us about the new urban planning policy.

e Perhaps they will have restrictions on the number of new homes.

f They complained that no one had followed the findings of their report.

Reading

3   Read the paragraph. Then answer the questions.

Twenty-three-year-old Katia moved from Sweden to England to work as an au pair with an English family for a year. 'I wanted to really immerse myself in the language and the culture, something you can't do as a tourist.' It was the first time she had lived apart from her family. 'I didn't realise how homesick I would be,' she remembers. 'At first, everything was exciting and new. I just wanted to go out and explore. But after about three months, I started to feel incredibly homesick. I missed my family and started looking for shops that sold food from home. I wondered if I had made a big mistake!' But the homesick phase didn't last long. 'Instead of complaining that things were different, I started looking for things to love, and that made a big difference.'

a   What is the main topic of this paragraph?
  A   How to adapt to living in another country
  B   Difficulties of living away from home
  C   Learning about your own cultural identity

b   What did the writer learn on her year abroad?
  A   There will always be things you miss from home.
  B   You need to accept things you don't like.
  C   You must look for positives in your new environment.

c   Do you have an experience of living or visiting a country with a different culture? What did you learn? Write about it in your notebook.

Writing

4   Choose one of the situations below. Write a report based on your experience and those of your classmates. Include recommendations on whether this class trip should be repeated and how it could be improved.

  a   *You live in a large city and went on a one-day class trip to the countryside to visit a farm.*

  Or

  b   *You live in the country and went on a one-day class trip to a large city.*

REFLECTION

Write answers to these questions in your notebook.

a   What do you think are the most important issues affecting migration today?

b   How would you describe your cultural identity?

c   Would you like to move to another country to live? What would you like or dislike about it?

d   What advice would you give to someone who came to live in your country?

e   What did you learn about report writing in this unit? How could you improve your report next time?

6 Technology: Love it or hate it?

Think about it: Space rules

1 **Match the two parts of each sentence to make definitions.**

a	Geostationary satellites	☐	are groups of satellites that deliver internet connections to Earth from space.
b	Internet coverage	☐	is a system of laws and agreements that control the use and exploration of space.
c	Satellite mega constellations	☐	is a journey into space by a manned or unmanned spacecraft.
d	Low Earth orbit means that it rotates	☐	is caused when reflections from satellites disrupt astronomical observations.
e	Light pollution	☐	is formed when pieces of defunct satellites gather together in one place.
f	Space junk	☐	is provided by several competing companies that operate groups of satellites.
g	Orbit congestion	☐	is the overcrowding of space, especially in the low orbit area.
h	A cloud of debris	☐	just a few hundred kilometres above the Earth.
i	A space mission	☐	refers to any pieces of debris from old satellites floating in space.
j	Space regulation	☐	rotate at a fixed position in high orbit above the Earth's surface.

2   **Read this article about satellites. Complete the table.**

Artificial satellites

Artificial satellites today are not only smaller, they are also cheaper to launch. As a result, the number of satellites has been rapidly increasing. Right now, there are over 4000 of them, with the largest being the International Space Station (ISS).

The size and altitude of a satellite depends on its purpose. Satellites that are used to provide internet and phone communications are usually in low orbit above the Earth (LEO). Their altitude varies from 200 km to 200,000 km and their orbit varies between 90 minutes to a few hours.

Weather satellites also operate at LEO so that they can cover every area of the Earth and produce more detailed images. They are used for Earth observation, monitoring clouds, water vapour and surface features.

The Global Positioning System (GPS) system utilises a set of 24 satellites at an altitude of 20,000 km above the Earth. Sets of signals from several satellites in the group are used to pinpoint the correct location on the Earth's surface for use by navigational devices in cars and planes. They orbit the earth every 12 hours.

Geostationary satellites are positioned at an altitude of over 36,000 km, where they can view the same location continuously. They orbit the Earth at the

International Space Station (ISS)

same length of time it takes the Earth to rotate so they look as if they are stationary. These satellites in geostationary orbit (GEO) are used to provide Earth observation images, as well as for weather and internet communication.

The ISS is a space laboratory where scientists can perform many research experiments in a microgravity environment. Its altitude is 400 km and it orbits the Earth once every 92 minutes.

Type of satellite	Altitude	Time of one orbit	Use/purpose
Low Earth orbit (LEO)			
International Space Station (ISS)			
Medium Earth orbit (MEO)			
Geostationary orbit (GEO)			

Challenge

3   **What are the advantages and disadvantages of having satellites in orbit around the Earth? Make a list in your notebook.**

Technology and computer science: Digital security

1   **What do you know about secret codes?**
    List three kinds of code that you have heard of.

    ....

2   **Read the article. Underline the words that are new to you.**
    Try to work out their meaning by looking at the context.

Cryptography: What is it and why do we need it?

What would you do if you wanted to send someone a secret message? Send it in code, of course! A code is basically a way of scrambling a message using a key that only the sender and the receiver know. If anyone else opens the message, it just looks like random letters or numbers.

Julius Caesar, a Roman general, famously used an alphabet code to transmit top secret messages to his army. He simply substituted each letter of the alphabet with another letter three places along. For example, the word today would look like this:

TODAY → QLAXV

Alphabet	A	B	C	D	E	F	G	H	I	J	K	L	M	N	O	P	Q	R	S	T	U	V	W	X	Y	Z
Cipher	X	Y	Z	A	B	C	D	E	F	G	H	I	J	K	L	M	N	O	P	Q	R	S	T	U	V	W

But what if someone discovered the key? What if they intercepted the message and worked out how to crack the code?

That is why **encryption** (putting a message into code) is so important on the internet. People often want to exchange information that is private and confidential, such as those for financial transactions, and they don't want hackers or others to be able to read it. There are two types of encryption used on the web: symmetric and asymmetric.

Symmetric encryption works in a similar way to the Caesar cipher described above. Both sender and receiver have a shared code that they use to encrypt and **decrypt** (read the message using the key) their messages. But there's a problem. How do you share the code securely, especially if you live miles away from each other?

Asymmetric encryption – also known as public key encryption – was designed as a way to solve this problem. The first step is for each person to use a computer program that generates two keys, a public key and a private key. The public key can be sent openly, but the private key is known only to the person who created it. The sender (A) and the receiver (B) both exchange their public keys. Person A then encrypts the message using B's public key and sends it to B. The only way to decrypt this message is by using B's private key.

Encryption is used on the internet for transmitting all kinds of sensitive, confidential or personal information and wherever identity verification is required. It's used on messaging platforms, in online banking and for online shopping. Undoubtedly, as hackers and cyber criminals develop ever more sophisticated tools to steal online data, the field of cryptography will continue to be an important and evolving science.

READING TIP

After you finish reading, try to summarise the main ideas in your head. For this article, imagine that you are explaining the process of encryption to a younger friend. How well can you explain it without looking at the text?

3 Reread the article and then answer these questions.

a What is cryptography?

....

b What are two problems with Caesar's code?

....

c How are symmetric and asymmetric encryption different from each other?

....

d Why is encryption needed on the web?

....

4 Create a flowchart to illustrate the process of asymmetric encryption. Draw it in your notebook.

Use of English: Words of negation

Facts about space

- There isn't any sound in space because there is no atmosphere.
- Human footprints on the Moon will not disappear because there is no wind there.
- Mercury, Venus and Mars have a rocky surface, but none of them are habitable.
- Not all planets have moons. Neither Mercury nor Venus has any moons.
- Space missions have visited Mars, but no human has set foot on the planet yet.

Check!

1 Read the facts about space and underline words of negation.

Notice

2 Which words are used to negate the following?

a a verb ....

b a quantifier ....

c a noun ....

d one thing ....

e two things ....

Focus

3 Circle the correct word to complete each sentence.

a There is *no / not* life on the Earth's moon.

b *No one / None* knows how many stars there are in space.

c *Neither / None* of the many space missions to Mars found any evidence of life.

d Pluto has two moons but *neither / none* of them looks like Earth's moon.

e *Not / No* all stars in the galaxy have planets that orbit around them.

Practice

4 Find and correct the mistakes in each sentence.

   a I haven't visited the new space museum not yet.

   b Any of my friends are interested in astronomy.

   c We don't know not much about other galaxies.

   d We cannot study neither astronomy nor meteorology at my school.

   e There isn't no one who has been to Pluto yet.

Challenge

5 Rewrite these sentences using the words provided.

   a Astronauts in space feel like they don't have any weight. (no)

   ....

   b Most of the astronauts on the space mission did a spacewalk. (not)

   ....

   c Mercury does not have any rings around it and Venus does not have any either. (neither)

   ....

   d Many messages have been transmitted into space, but there haven't been any replies. (no)

   ....

   e There are seven other planets in our solar system, but they aren't habitable. (none)

   ....

GET IT RIGHT!

Be careful not to include two negatives in the same sentence as it creates a double negative.

Examples:
*We don't want to change **anything** in our classroom.* (not *nothing*)

*You shouldn't miss **any** of your lessons.* (not *none*)

*I don't have **any** time to talk right now.* (not *no time*)

Use of English: Defining and non-defining relative clauses

USE OF ENGLISH

There are many kinds of robots which are used in healthcare nowadays. A hospital cleaning robot, which uses UV rays, can disinfect a whole room in just a few minutes. Other types of robot can scan patients' physical symptoms, which saves time for the doctor or nurse. The data which they collect can also be stored and searched more easily. There are surgical robots whose purpose is to provide greater precision during surgeries. Surgeons who use these robots can make more precise incisions that will benefit the patient by healing more quickly.

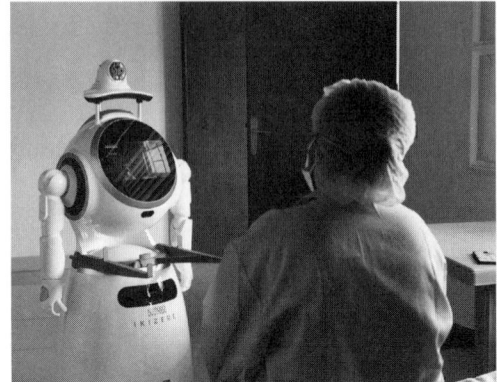

Check!

1   Read the text about healthcare robots. Underline the relative pronouns.

2   Circle the word or phrase in the text that each relative pronoun refers to.

Notice

3   Which of the relative pronouns in the text...

   a   can be replaced with *that*   ....

   b   can be omitted   ....

   c   refers to a whole clause   ....

   d   uses commas   ....

Focus

4   Match the two parts of each sentence.

   a   There is a robot which   can have access to healthcare through telerobots.

   b   Surgical robots are more accurate,   help the doctors to provide better care.

   c   Robots can clean hospital rooms   is designed to deliver injections and other therapies.

   d   Patients who live far away from a hospital   which has helped reduce the number of errors.

   e   The tasks that robots carry out in hospital   which reduces the risk of infections.

Practice

5 Find and correct the errors. Replace *which* with *that*, if possible. One sentence is correct.

a   Healthcare robots can save time and money which makes them very popular.

b   Patient data is collected and stored, that means it can be used for future research.

c   The cost of medicine is rising that makes it difficult for some countries to buy them.

d   Surgeries that are performed by surgical robots have a low risk of errors.

e   Robots have been designed to help care for patients at home, which reduces their hospital time.

Challenge

6 Complete the text by writing each relative clause a–h in the best place. Add the correct relative pronoun. Use *that* and omit the relative pronoun when possible.

Wearable health trackers are changing our attitudes to healthcare. A band

....[1] monitors your heart rate and

blood pressure, ...[2]. It can collect

data over a period of time, ...[3] of

your overall health. Fitness trackers can check how much exercise you do

and will send messages ....[4]. People

....[5] can also use a wearable device to

monitor their blood glucose levels. Instead of testing tiny blood samples,

....[6], the wristband has sensors

....[7] from fluids in the body. This kind of

technology, ...[8] on individual engagement,

is making people more aware of their health and how to stay healthy.

a   can be unpleasant
b   can have many health benefits
c   collect glucose samples
d   have diabetes
e   presents a more accurate picture
f   remind you to exercise more
g   places more emphasis
h   that you wear on your wrist

GET IT RIGHT!

Notice that *which* can be used to refer back to a complete clause. In this case, it is a non-defining clause. If a comma is required, the word *which* cannot be replaced by *that* and the verb is singular.

Example:
I exercise daily and eat lots of fresh vegetables, which keeps me very healthy. (*Which* refers back to the whole clause and a comma is required.)

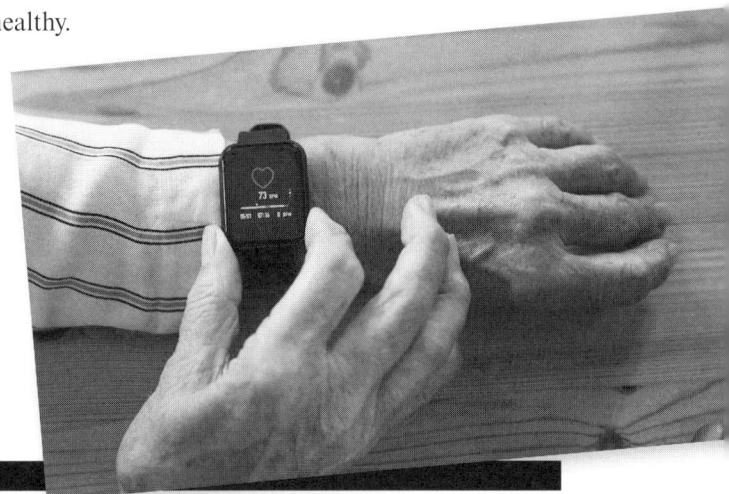

Academic writing: For and against essay

1   **Look at the photo. Think of two different ways of interpreting the photo. Write your ideas below.**

a   someone who loves social media

....

b   someone who dislikes social media.

....

LANGUAGE TIP

Language of contrast and disagreement

Expressions of contrast can help signal to the reader the kind of information that is coming next. These expressions can show contrast within a sentence or across sentences. Compare these two examples.

__Although__ many people enjoy using social media, it can also have some negative effects. (*Although* introduces the first clause, while the second clause presents the opposing argument.)

Many people enjoy using social media. __However,__ it can also have some negative effects. (*However* introduces a new sentence with a contrasting idea to the previous sentence and uses a comma.)

---

2   **Circle the correct word to complete each sentence.**

a   Technology can help students with remote learning, *although / however* it reduces face to face interactions.

b   *While / Nevertheless* everyone has more opportunities to socialise online, many people feel isolated.

c   There are many reasons why companies collect data from online consumers. *However, / Although* some people are worried that it invades our privacy.

d   It is important to be careful about transmitting private data online. *Even though / Nonetheless,* encrypted websites offer some degree of security.

3   Read the essay question. Then complete the graphic organiser with your ideas about the topic. Consider the questions in the box to help you.

Social media offers many positive opportunities to interact with other people, but some people believe it can have negative effects as well. What are the arguments for and against the use of social media?

- How does social media help people stay in touch?
- In what situations is it better than other forms of communication?
- How does it influence our friendships?
- Why is online bullying a problem?
- Why can social media sometimes make people anxious or depressed?
- Can social media be overused?

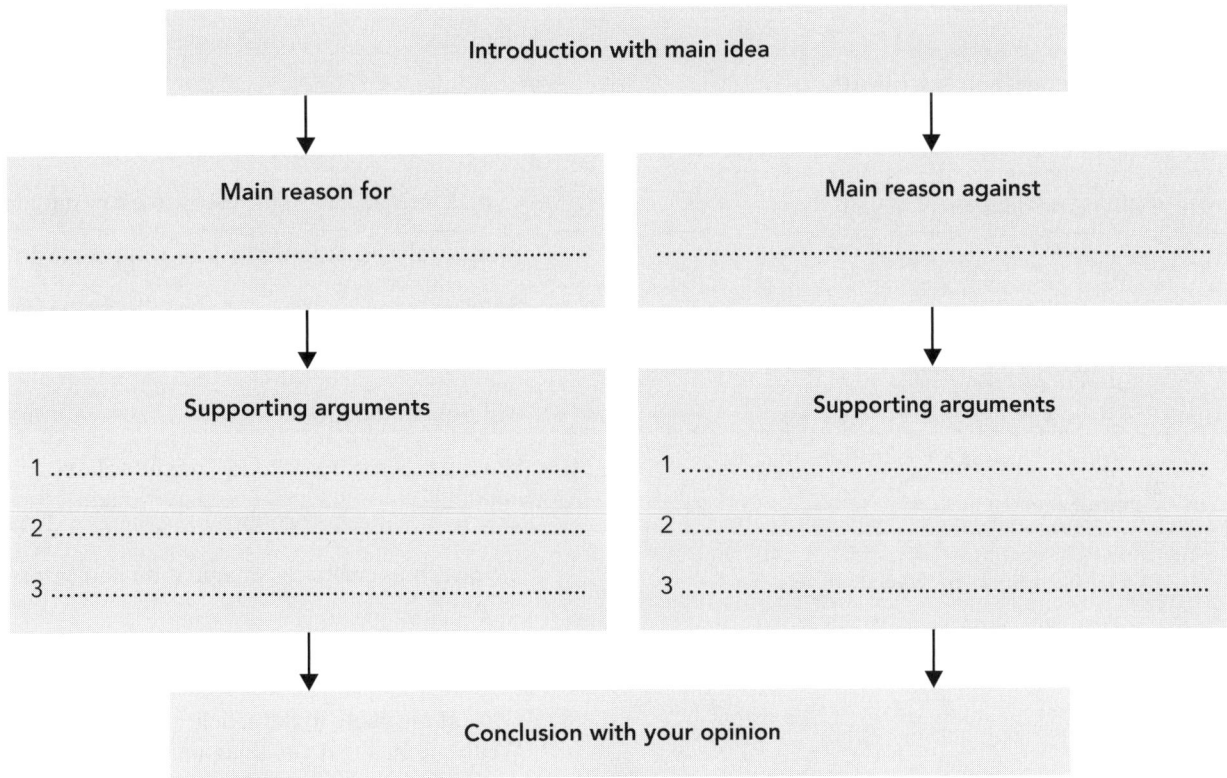

Introduction with main idea

Main reason for

....

Main reason against

....

Supporting arguments

1 ....
2 ....
3 ....

Supporting arguments

1 ....
2 ....
3 ....

Conclusion with your opinion

4   Use your notes from Exercise 3 to write an essay to answer the question.

Check your progress

Vocabulary

1   **Circle the correct word(s) to complete each sentence.**

   a   Geostationary satellites orbit the Earth at
       low / high altitudes.

   b   A cloud of debris is a collection of pieces of
       rocks / satellites.

   c   Satellite mega constellations are
       large satellites / groups of satellites.

   d   Orbit congestion describes the
       overcrowding / organisation of space.

   e   Biometric data refers to your
       personal / physical details.

   f   An algorithm is a set of
       instructions / computers.

   g   Ultrasonic waves are vibrations that we
       cannot *see / hear.*

   h   Cryptography is the science of
       coding / transmitting data.

Grammar

2   **Use negative words or relative pronouns to complete the text. Use *that* or – (for a relative pronoun that can be omitted) where possible.**

There are ....¹ many jobs nowadays ....² don't involve some use of technology. It's hard to imagine a world that has ....³ computers. And computers are getting faster and smarter all the time, ...⁴ makes some people worry that they will replace humans. In the world of the future, where workplaces are full of robots ....⁵ purpose is to carry out most routine jobs, what kinds of jobs will people do? Surely ....⁶ all skills can be learned by robots? The skills ....⁷ humans will need in the future, ...⁸ may be very different from today, might well be skills ....⁹ robots ....¹⁰ have, such as creativity, imagination and empathy.

Reading

3   **Look at the photo in the article on the next page. Write one idea that you think may be in the article.**

....

....

....

....

4 **Read the article and choose the best title.**

A Why you should have a smart home

B Is a smart home for you?

C A smart home – pros and cons

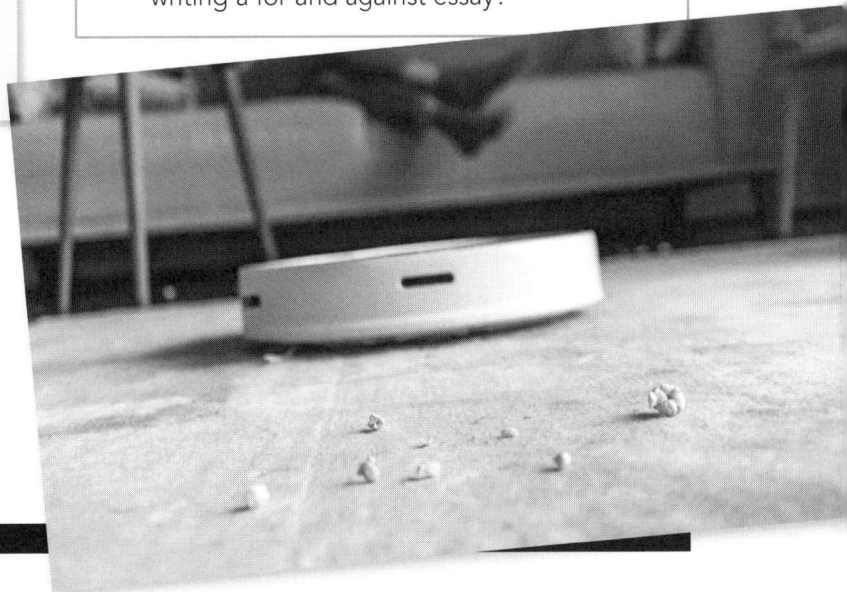

How can you turn your home into a 'smart home'? It's easy! But first, let's define the meaning of smart home. Basically, it's any home that is equipped with devices that do tasks automatically or which can be operated remotely. These devices can be operated by a switch, an app or a voice command. A wide range of equipment, from cameras and computers to lighting and heating, can all be linked through one remote operation. By recognising your daily routines, lights and heating will automatically turn down when you don't need them. Cameras and sensors can monitor your home while you're away and send you alerts. Household appliances can also be linked in, with a robot vacuum cleaner, a fridge that alerts you when you're running out of milk and an oven that starts cooking dinner in time for when you arrive home.

5 **What do you think is the purpose of this article?**

A to explain how a smart home works

B to persuade you to have a smart home

C to describe a typical smart home

6 **Summarise three ways that smart home technology can improve your life.**

....

....

....

Writing

7 **Read the essay question and make notes for and against. Write the essay in your notebook.**

Some people think that technology has made it easier for people to study remotely and that there is no longer any need for students to attend school in person. Others believe that vital skills will be lost. What are the arguments for and against remote learning?

REFLECTION

Write answers to these questions in your notebook.

a What aspects of technology mentioned in this unit are you most interested in?

b What facts about satellites and fingerprint scanning did you learn that you didn't know before?

c List three ways in which technology has changed in the last five years. What effects has it had?

d What is the most important way you use technology in your daily life?

e What did you find most challenging about writing a for and against essay?

7 Social inequality

Think about it: Stereotypes in video games

1   Match the words with the examples.

> bias   diversity   gender discrimination   injustice
> prejudice   racism   stereotype

a   The school committee decided to suspend the student even though he hadn't done anything wrong. ……………………

b   This newspaper tends to have articles that lean towards the left-wing side of the political debate. ……………………

c   A teacher gave higher marks to male students than to female students even if their work was not as good. ……………………

d   People used to think that girls should play with dolls, and boys with toy cars and trucks. ……………………

e   The company set a goal for employing people from a wide range of ethnic backgrounds. ……………………

f   He went to a famous university, so he is certainly the best person for this job. ……………………

g   The company promoted a white candidate at work even though some Asian and black candidates had better qualifications. ……………………

2 **Read the article and answer the questions.**

Gender-neutral language

Although we may not always be aware of them, our unconscious biases can affect the way we think and how we interact with other people. Unconscious stereotypes can also be embedded in the language we use. Some nouns for occupations are assumed to be male unless explicitly marked as female. An *actor,* for example, is expected to be male, because a female would be described as an *actress.* Similarly, with words like *police officer* or *judge*, a female is described as a *woman police officer* or a *female judge.* In other words, male is assumed to be normal and female is the exception. Other gender stereotypes emerge when we use words for occupations such as *doctor or engineer*, which have traditionally been male dominated. We tend to assume they are male, whereas *teacher* or *nurse* or *secretary* are usually assumed to be female. To counter this kind of biased thinking, people are seeking more gender-neutral terms. Words like *chairman* or *postman* can easily be changed to *chairperson* or *postal worker.* Others discourage the use of *woman or female* to qualify a noun and instead are working to change perceptions, so that words like *politician or president* become more gender inclusive.

a The article describes three ways that words for occupations illustrate bias. What are they?

....

....

....

b Why do some people object to the term *woman police officer*?

....

c What is a gender-neutral term?

....

d What is a gender-inclusive term?

....

e Do you agree that these terms encourage gender-biased thinking? How could they impact equal opportunities for everyone?

....

Challenge

3 **What are some ways that gender stereotypes are embedded in your language? What can be done to change them? Write three ideas in your notebook.**

History: Children in the workforce

1   Look at the photo. What kind of work do you think children did in Europe in the 18th and 19th centuries? Write three ideas.

....

....

....

2   Read the article and check your answer to Exercise 1.

Child labour during the Industrial Revolution

A   Child labour is often defined as work that is mentally or physically harmful to children and prevents them from going to school. Whether they are paid or not, if their work produces something that can be sold, it is considered to be child labour.

B   In the agricultural communities of Europe before the Industrial Revolution, child labour was considered normal. Children as young as five would work in the fields planting or harvesting crops. They also helped with domestic production (known as cottage industries) such as weaving or making clothes. In urban areas, boys worked as chimney sweeps or were apprenticed to learn a trade, while girls were expected to find work as maidservants in wealthier households.

C   With the onset of the Industrial Revolution at the end of the 18th century, factory and mine owners were eager to hire children as part of their workforce. Children were small and agile, which made them ideal for climbing around factory machinery in cotton mills or into narrow mining tunnels. Not only that, they could also be paid less than adults, which generated greater profits for the factory owners.

D   However, the work was dangerous, and children were often in danger of severe harm from machine accidents. They worked long hours, sometimes as many as 60 hours a week, and were poorly paid. Living conditions were overcrowded and unsanitary, which contributed to shorter life expectancy. Food and rent were deducted from their pay, so they earned very little.

E   Around the end of the 18th century and beginning of the 19th century, social reformers started to investigate the dangerous working conditions for children. Laws such as the Factory Acts of 1802 and 1819 in England attempted to restrict the working hours of children in factories and cotton mills to 12 hours per day, but there were so many loopholes in the laws that they had little effect.

F   It was only towards the second half of the 19th century that numbers of child labourers started to decline. There were several reasons for this. One was that technology improved, so that many simple jobs could be performed by machines. There was also a need for more skilled workers. Therefore, it was more economically advantageous for workers to attend school and be educated. This eventually led to the introduction of compulsory education, which ensured that every child had the right to go to school.

> **READING TIP**
>
> After you finish each paragraph, try to summarise the main idea in your head.
> This will help you to follow and understand the writer's argument.

3 Match these subheadings to the correct paragraphs in the passage.
Write the correct letter, A–F.

a   How did people try to improve working conditions for children?   ....

b   What is child labour?   ....

c   What kind of work did children do before the Industrial Revolution?   ....

d   What were the dangers endured by child labourers?   ....

e   Why did numbers of child labourers start to fall?   ....

f   Why were children employed during the Industrial Revolution?   ....

4 Find these sentences in the passage. What do the words in bold refer back to?

a   Whether **they** are paid or not   ....

b   **which** contributed to shorter life expectancy.   ....

c   there were so many loopholes that **they** had little effect.   ....

d   There were several reasons for **this.**   ....

5 Rephrase the words in bold using your own words.

a   **maidservant** in wealthier households.   ....

b   shorter **life expectancy**   ....

c   **social reformers**   ....

d   **loopholes**   ....

6 Summarise the main points of the passage in this chart.

Before the Industrial Revolution	During the Industrial Revolution	After the Industrial Revolution

Use of English: Adverbs of manner, degree and focus

USE OF ENGLISH

University applications have fallen dramatically this year, primarily because tuition fees rose sharply in September. The total number of applicants was down approximately 8% on the previous year. Some students are increasingly worried about the prospect of taking on too much debt. Others say that the job market has improved steadily over the past year and the number of well-paid jobs that don't require a university degree has increased significantly. Clearly, the increased cost of going to university will mostly affect students from lower-income backgrounds and may especially impact their chances of social mobility and future earning power. Several studies have shown that students who do not continue education after secondary school are likely to earn substantially less than those who go on to earn a bachelor's degree.

Check!

1   Read the text and underline the adverbs of manner, degree and focus. Then write them in the correct place.

Adverbs of manner (how something changed): ....

Adverbs of degree (intensity of the change):

....

Adverbs of focus (focus attention on a particular part of the sentence):

....

Notice

2   Which adverb does not fit any of the categories? ....

Focus

3   Circle the correct phrase to complete each sentence.

a   There .... five people per visit.

can exactly be   can be exactly   exactly can be

b   Response to the new government loan scheme .... positive.

mostly was positive   was positive mostly   was mostly positive

c   Unemployment figures .... in the first quarter of the year.

have fallen dramatically   dramatically have fallen   have dramatically fallen

d   There has been .... increase in the number of part-time students.

a reasonably steady   reasonably a steady   a reasonable

Practice

4   Rewrite the sentences using adverbs from the Language tip box.

a   It appears that the number of people in full-time study has risen.

....

b   Anyone can see that equal access to education should be a priority.

....

c   It is no surprise that students are more motivated when they have clear career goals.

....

d   It was ironic that the number of nurses fell just as the pandemic started.

....

> **LANGUAGE TIP**
>
> Some adverbs can be used at the beginning of a sentence to indicate the writer's attitude to the whole sentence.
>
> Example:
> *Clearly, this price increase will have a negative impact.*
> (I think it is clear that this price increase will have a negative impact.)
>
> Other adverbs that can be used in this manner include: *apparently, essentially, evidently, ironically, interestingly, obviously, surprisingly, unsurprisingly, understandably.*

Challenge

5   Complete the paragraph using words from the box.

> clearly   crucially   especially   exactly   fully   greatly
> obviously   significantly   slightly   surprisingly

Equality in education is ....[1] an important step on the path towards social equality. But the concept of educational equality, perhaps not ....[2], can be interpreted in ....[3] different ways. First, there is the idea of sameness, meaning that everyone has access to ....[4] the same resources and opportunities. Another interpretation, sometimes called equity, refers to fairness. ....[5], different students can have ....[6] different needs. Equity means that every child receives the educational support they need to ....[7] achieve their potential. Equality and equity are both ....[8] important to ensuring student success. In practice, they can have ....[9] different implications ....[10] when it comes to educational policy and planning.

Use of English: Comparing statistics

Which occupations are dominated by males or by females?

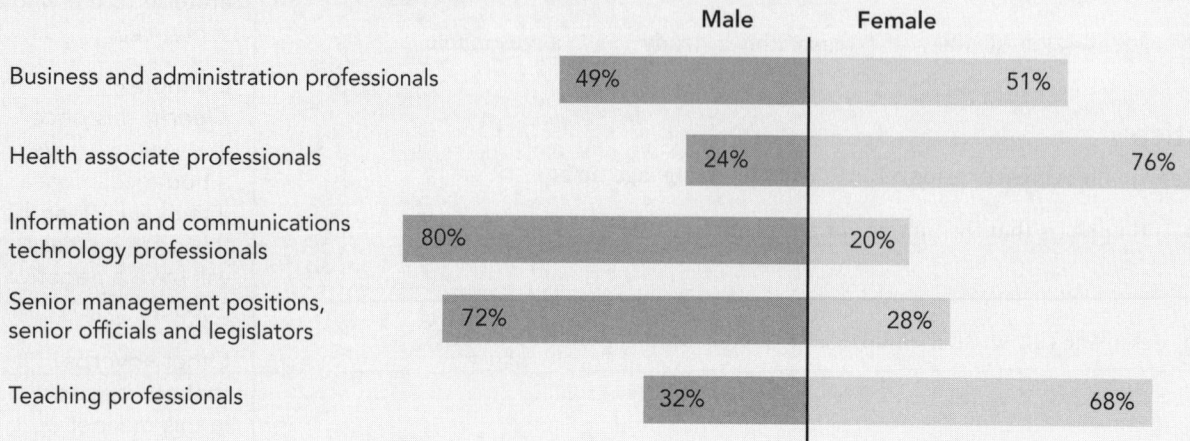

	Male	Female
Business and administration professionals	49%	51%
Health associate professionals	24%	76%
Information and communications technology professionals	80%	20%
Senior management positions, senior officials and legislators	72%	28%
Teaching professionals	32%	68%

Note: The weighted average is not a global figure. It is based on available data for 121 countries, which represent 63% of global employment. Data for China and India were not available. Source: International Labour Organization

The data showed that male workers were **just as likely as** female workers to have jobs in business and administration. Female workers were **three times more likely than** male workers to work in health care professions. There were **four times as many** male workers in IT jobs than female. There were **two and a half times as many males as** females in senior management. The number of females who became teachers was **twice as high as** the number of males.

Check!

1   Read the information about gender differences in occupations.
    What do the phrases in bold have in common?

    ....

2   Do you think these averages are true in your country?
    Draw a star next to the ones that might be different.

Notice

3   Look at each comparison. When do we use *as*? When do we use *than*?

    ....

Focus

4   Complete the sentences with words from the box.

as   longer   many   much   than

a   I have to work twice as hard in my new job .... in my last job.

b   My salary is three times higher .... yours.

c   There are twice as .... female employees as male employees.

d   I have to work .... hours than many of my colleagues.

e   We have .... more flexibility in this company than in my previous job.

Practice

5   **Find and correct the mistake in each sentence. One sentence is correct.**

a   Filling out the application forms took ten times longer as I had expected.

b   Students who completed university earned a salary that was three times high as those who did not.

c   Younger students were three times likely to take out student loans than older ones.

d   The number of applications is two-thirds lower than the year before.

e   Female candidates were twice more successful in the exams as male applicants.

Challenge

6   **Write sentences in your notebook to compare each set of data using the structures from this lesson.**

Company annual report: Human resources		
	2012	2022
a Male employees	500	250
b Female employees	300	100
c Average salary per month	$300	$400
d Average hours per week worked from home	12	16
e Average number of sick days per employee	9	6

GET IT RIGHT!

When making comparisons between sets of data, we can use these two different structures:

- x is/are (half, twice, three times, etc.) as (adjective) as y

  Example: *Jobs in IT **are twice as** well-paid **as** jobs in education.*

- x is/are (three times, four times, etc.) (comparative form) than y.

  Example: *Study places for science degrees **are ten times more numerous than** for arts degrees.*

Academic writing: Describing data in a table

1   Change the words in bold so that they are more academic. Use words from the box.

> dramatically   particularly   reasonably   significant   slightly

   a   There was a **big** increase in employment over the last six months.

   b   The numbers of adults in full-time education decreased **a little bit**.

   c   The fall in interest rates caused borrowing to increase **a lot**.

   d   The rise in consumer confidence was **really** noticeable.

   e   The rate of inflation was **quite** low compared to the previous quarter.

2   **Look at the title of the table.**

   What do you think are some of the reasons for children not going to primary school?

   ....

Share of primary-school-age children who are not in school		
Region	1999	2019
World	16%	8%
Sub-Saharan Africa	41%	19%
South Asia	23%	7%
Middle East and North Africa	16%	5%
East Asia and Pacific	5%	3%
Latin America and Caribbean	4%	3%
Europe and Central Asia	3%	2%
North America	2%	0.5%

3   **Look at the table again. Answer these questions.**

   a   What is the main topic of the table?

   ....

   b   What is the overall trend shown by the data?

   ....

   c   What does each row of the table show?

   ....

d   What does each column of the table show?

....

e   Compare the current and previous numbers for:

   i   the world ....

   ii   South Asia ....

   iii   Sub-Saharan Africa. ....

f   Which regions had a dramatic decrease?

....

g   Which regions had a slight decrease?

....

h   Would you say that the overall trend is positive or negative?

....

....

4   **Read the question. Use your notes from Exercise 3 to write a description of the table in your notebook.**

The table shows the percentage of primary school students in the world who didn't go to primary school in 1999 and 2019. Summarise the information by selecting and reporting the main features. Make comparisons where relevant.

> **WRITING TIP**
>
> When describing a table, it is a good idea to start with the general topic and overview, before going into the details.

Check your progress

Vocabulary

1 **Read the clues and complete the puzzle. Find the hidden word and write a definition for it.**

1 the place where you work
2 unfair treatment
3 having people from a variety of backgrounds
4 lack of fairness
5 having the same rights
6 male is one of these
7 a tendency to have certain opinions
8 negative attitudes to people of other races
9 a fixed image of people from a particular group

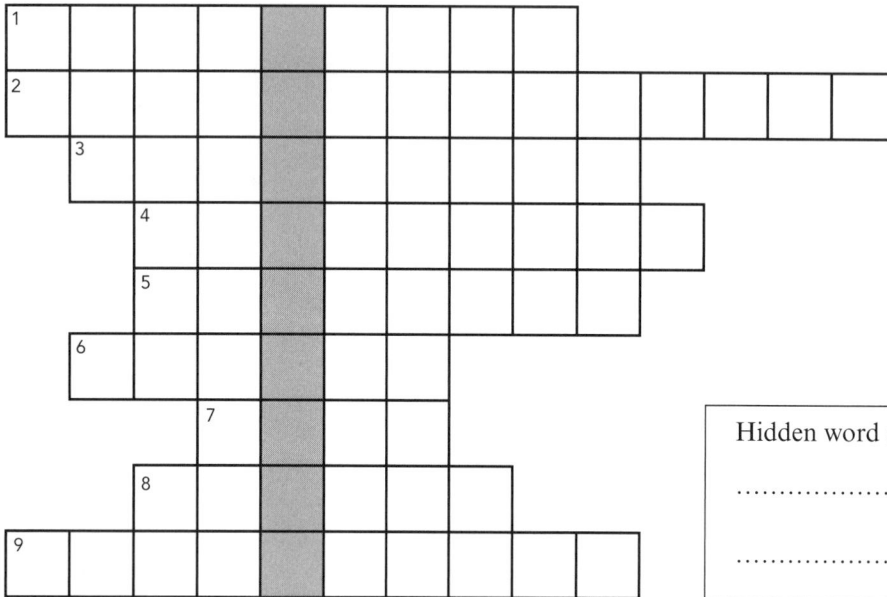

Hidden word and definition:

....

....

Grammar

2 **Circle the best words to complete the text.**

Quarterly Employment Report: The national employment report for this quarter shows that the number of new jobs rose *dramatically / clearly*[1]. *Evidently / Understandably*[2], employers are seeking to hire more workers, *basically / especially*[3] those that have tech and IT skills. Employment figures also increased *steadily / mostly*[4] over the previous quarter, with almost *twice / half*[5] as many new jobs in the restaurant and hospitality sector *as / than*[6] in the other service sectors. The number of unemployment claims remained low, with *primarily / approximately*[7] the same number of people claiming benefits *as / than*[8] in the previous quarter.

Reading

3   Read the text and answer the questions that follow.

Discrimination can happen anywhere: at school, in the playground, in the cafeteria or online. All kinds of discrimination are unfair and hurtful. But what can we do about **it**? [A] If you feel that you are being verbally attacked or bullied, you should talk to a teacher or a guidance counsellor. It is **their** duty to make sure that the school is a safe place for everyone. [B] If you see others who are behaving unfairly, say something to **them** or to a teacher. Think carefully about the language you use and stop using names and jokes **that** express negative stereotypes. [C] Finally, on a wider level, organise events or meetings where ways to combat discrimination are actively discussed. [D]

a   Who do you think the text is written for?

   A   teachers   **B**   parents   **C**   students

b   Where does this sentence fit in the text? Write the letter of the best place, A, B, C or D.   ....

   Being aware of our own prejudices is one step towards changing them.

c   What do the words in bold refer to?

   i   it ....   **ii**   their ....

   iii   them ....   **iv**   that ....

Writing

4   Write a brief description of the data in the table. Write about 150 words in your notebook.

Global Wealth Distribution 2021

Wealth range	Wealth	Global share (%)	Adult population
Over $1 million	$191.6 trillion	45.8%	Held by 1.1%
$100,000–$1 million	$163.9 trillion	39.1%	Held by 11.1%
$10,000–$100,000	$57.3 trillion	13.7%	Held by 32.8%
Less than $10,000	$5.5 trillion	1.3%	Held by 55.0%
Total	**$418.3 trillion**	**100.0%**	**Held by 100.0%**

Source: Visual Capitalist website

REFLECTION

Write answers to these questions in your notebook.

a   How has this unit widened your view of social inequality?

b   List five key words or phrases that you associate with the topic of this unit. Why did you choose them?

c   List three ways in which you think social inequality is changing.

d   What kinds of inequality are there in your country? How can they be changed?

e   List three positive things we can do in our daily lives to combat discrimination against others.

8 Arts and culture

Think about it: The power of drama

1 Read about three teenagers talking about their favourite television dramas.
Which one interests you most and why?

Mina: My favourite TV drama series is set in Italy in the 1950s. It tells the story of a friendship between two girls who grow up in a poor neighbourhood. Based on a best-selling novel, this drama has a **compelling** plot and fascinating characters. The sumptuous cinematography and **meticulously** recreated scenes of the past add to its magnetic visual appeal.

Anusha: This highly successful costume drama tells the story of an English **aristocratic** family and their servants. Starting in the early 20th century, the narrative revolves around romantic and political plots and subplots that reflect the background of the times. It presents an affectionately romantic view of the past that provides a **comforting** form of escapism.

Lucas: The scenario of this post-apocalyptic cli-fi series takes place after a nuclear apocalypse has made the Earth **uninhabitable**. The only human survivors live on space stations that were in orbit at the time of the disaster. However, when resources on board begin to **dwindle**, a group of people are sent to Earth to find out whether the atmosphere is habitable. They soon discover that there are other survivors and they will have to make tough decisions to fight sinister forces of evil.

....

2 Which teenager describes a TV series that does the following?

		Mina	Anusha	Lucas
a	is set in the future	☐	☐	☐
b	is very realistic	☐	☐	☐
c	is about wealthy people	☐	☐	☐
d	is a dystopian drama	☐	☐	☐
e	is about adolescence	☐	☐	☐
f	is set more than 100 years ago	☐	☐	☐
g	addresses themes of right and wrong	☐	☐	☐
h	could teach you about history	☐	☐	☐

3   **Match the words in bold in Exercise 1 with the correct meaning.**

a   cannot support human life ....

b   become scarce ....

c   upper class ....

d   done with careful attention to detail ....

e   reassuring ....

f   fascinating ....

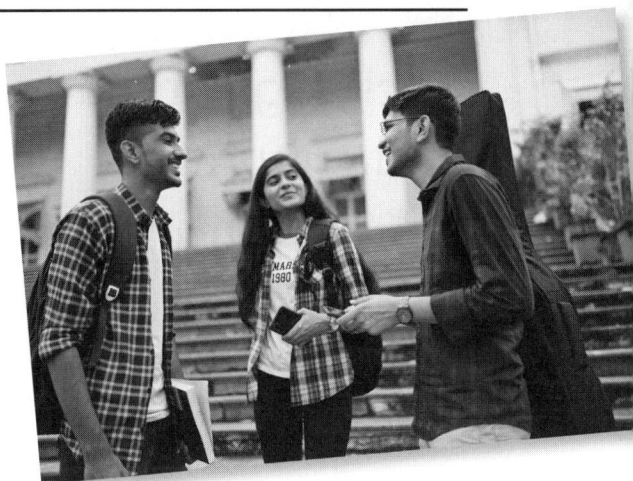

4   **Complete these opinions using words from the text in Exercise 1.**
Then write your own opinion about the type of TV series that you like.

I like
........................[1] that are
set in the future, but I don't like them if they
are too scary or ....[2]. Some of the
........................[3] genre TV shows are
so negative!

My
favourite kind of TV
dramas are ....[4] in the
past. They have a lot of ....[5]
because the fashions and homes are so attractive,
and it's quite ....[6] to imagine
a lifestyle that was somehow
simpler.

I don't like TV series that have lots of
........................[7] plots. I prefer action
and adventure, but there has to be an interesting
........................[8] too.

I usually go for sci-fi
series that are about space, or life
on earth after an ....[9] disaster.
Some of them are very ....[10] and
show things that could definitely happen
to us.

Your opinion: ....

Challenge

5   **Write a brief description of a TV series that you enjoyed watching.**
Write 80–100 words in your notebook.

Sociology and education: The impact of arts and culture

1 **Match the paragraphs in the article below with the questions they answer. Then write them in the correct place.**

Are there any career benefits of entering art competitions?

What are the social benefits of entering art competitions?

Why should I enter an art contest?

Are there any negatives of entering online competitions?

What if I have never had any art training?

How much does it cost?

What if my art isn't good enough?

What other kinds of online competitions are there?

Entering an international youth art competition

Have you ever thought about entering an online art competition? It's a great way to increase your confidence and expand your portfolio. Here are some frequently asked questions that may help you decide whether to enter your work or not.

....

The best reason for entering an art contest is to help you to grow as an artist. Creating an artwork for a contest challenges you to do your best as you know that judges will be evaluating your work. You'll get expert feedback from the judges, which will help you improve on your work.

....

There are many contests online that don't charge anything for submitting an entry. Some contests even offer a monetary prize for the winner and runners-up, so you may end up making some extra money to spend on art materials.

....

It doesn't matter! Art contests are open to everyone, regardless of their social, cultural or educational background. However, you should check the rules and regulations carefully as some contests may have age limits or may restrict entries to certain countries.

....

That's exactly why you should give it a try! If you don't win first time, you can improve and try again. That is how you will gain self-esteem and faith in yourself as an artist.

....

By entering a contest, you become part of a community of artists and can network with other artists who have similar interests. Perhaps you have been working alone with no one to share your work with. This a great way to join a supportive artist community. You can develop your ideas and improve your ability to convey them to others as well.

....

As always, you should beware of **scams** and fakes. Always read the competition information carefully. Make sure that the organisation is a non-profit and not a private company or individual trying to make money from artists' work. You should also verify who will own the **copyright** on your artwork after you send it in and whether it will be used to promote other products or activities without your knowledge.

....

It can be helpful to mention that you have entered or won an art competition on your resume or in your art **portfolio**. If you win,

your work will be published in an online art show catalogue and you can start to build your name recognition.

....

Art is not the only way to enter an online competition. There are contests for photography, writing, graphic design and fashion as well as competitions that combine art with science or maths and involve skills such as critical thinking, communication, collaboration and creativity. To get started, search our list of links to free online competitions.

---

scam: a dishonest or fraudulent scheme

copyright: the right to maintain control of your own work

portfolio: a selection of your work that can be used to assess performance or skill

---

2   **Write the phrases or sentences in the text that refer to the following.**

a   community cohesion   ....

b   confidence and motivation   ....

c   communication skills   ....

d   critically evaluating a text ....

e   social competency   ....

f   level playing field   ....

g   social isolation   ....

h   STEAM skills   ....

Challenge

3   **Have you ever entered an online contest? How did you feel about entering? What did you learn from it? If you have never entered a contest, write about why you would or would not like to enter one. Write a short entry in your notebook.**

Use of English: *-ing* and *-ed* adjectives

USE OF ENGLISH

Check!

1 Read the conversation. Underline the *-ed* and *-ing* adjectives.

Notice

2 Which adjectives describe emotions, or how people feel? ....

3 Which adjectives describe the thing or person that causes the emotion? ....

Focus

4 Match the two parts of each sentence.

a	I have read this book three times	i	which was really entertaining.
b	The film has a sad ending,	ii	because he was terribly tired.
c	We laughed all the way through the show,	iii	so everyone was very excited.
d	The concert was cancelled at the last minute	iv	because it is so inspiring.
e	There was a chance to get free tickets	v	which is quite depressing.
f	He fell asleep during the play	vi	so they were terribly disappointed.

Practice

5   Circle the correct word to complete each sentence.

a   Performing on stage for the first time was a *terrified / terrifying* experience.

b   The *amused / amusing* dialogue in this book often made me laugh out loud.

c   The actors went home after a long day of *tired / tiring* rehearsals.

d   I didn't understand and looked at her with a *puzzled / puzzling* expression.

e   The most *interesting / interested* thing about the film was its ending.

f   The conductor bowed to the audience with a *satisfying / satisfied* smile.

Challenge

6   Complete the text with the correct *-ing* or *-ed* form of the adjectives in the box. Use the words in the same order they are provided.

excite   thrill   amaze   fascinate   impress   refresh
inspire   interest   relax   stun   tire   disappoint

> **GET IT RIGHT!**
>
> Both *-ed* and *-ing* adjectives can be used before a noun. Use *-ing* adjectives when the person or thing causes the emotion. Use *-ed* adjectives when the adjective describes an emotion experienced by a person.
>
> Examples: *There was **a surprising twist** in the story.* (The twist caused a surprise.)
>
> *After five hours of rehearsals, **the exhausted travellers** arrived.* (The travellers felt exhausted.)

Art and culture day trip

Join us for an ....[1] programme of cultural and arts activities in London this weekend. We are sure you will be ....[2] by the ....[3] itinerary we have put together for you. Our first stop will be the British Museum, where we will visit ....[4] exhibits from ancient Rome. No one can fail to be ....[5] by the extraordinary beauty of these ancient artefacts. After that, we will stop for a ....[6] walk through Hyde Park, before taking a light lunch in the garden café. After lunch, we will visit the Tate Modern art museum for an ....[7] lecture on 20th-century art, and afterwards those who are ....[8] can explore the modern art collection. After a ....[9] tea in the museum café, we will go to the Cambridge Theatre for a ....[10] performance of *Les Misérables*. After the show, those who are not too ....[11] may want to go out for dinner. We are sure you will not be ....[12] by your day or arts and culture in the city.

Use of English: Cleft sentences

Tell us about your favourite fantasy fiction. Post your comments here.

☐ What I really love about this series is the way characters are forced to confront good and evil.

☐ The best thing about this book is that you can escape into a completely different world.

☐ The reason why these books are so successful is because they focus mainly on the characters.

☐ It is the friendships between the characters that make this story so timeless.

☐ What really fascinates me about these books is the detailed creation of an imaginary world.

☐ The character I love the most in this book is the old man because he's so wise and good.

☐ What makes these books so amazing is the sense of eternal values like courage and bravery.

Check!

1 Read the blog comments above and underline the key information in each sentence.

2 Circle the correct word to complete each sentence.

   a We use 'What… is…' and 'The thing about x is that…' to signal that the key point will come *first / later* in the sentence.

   b We use 'It is… that' to signal that the key point will come *first / later* in the sentence.

Notice

3 Which of the blog comments have a cleft sentence that refers to an object? Tick the answers. Notice the position of the subject.

Focus

4 **Rewrite each sentence with a cleft sentence structure using the words provided.**

   a I really love the soundtrack to this film.

   What ....

b   I didn't like the final scene. But everything else was good.

The only ....

c   The descriptions of the characters in this book are truly extraordinary.

It ....

d   I found the frequent plot twists to be quite confusing.

What ....

e   The series was very popular because of the historical setting.

The reason ....

Practice

5   **Find and correct the errors. One sentence is correct.**

a   What I enjoyed most about the book it was the funny dialogue.

b   It was watching the TV series made me interested in reading the books.

c   What makes the paintings so unusual are the use of light and dark.

d   The only reason I watched the film was that it was set in Iceland.

e   The books readers liked them the best were the ones about mystery and adventure.

6   **Complete the text using words in the box.**

what	is	it	that	the	things	what	that

TV review of the week: This new TV drama series is based on a series of popular fantasy books. ....¹ makes this series so compelling is its richly imagined characters and dramatic plot. The reason for its popularity is ....² every episode is full of action and drama. But ....³ is the characters and their motivations that drive the plot. Although they live in a fantasy world, ...⁴ matters is ....⁵ we can easily relate to them. One of ....⁶ most impressive ....⁷ about this series ....⁸ its use of visual effects for which the creators have won several awards.

Challenge

7   **Think of a TV series that you enjoyed. Write a review in your notebook. Use at least three cleft sentences in your description.**

LANGUAGE TIP

When the introductory noun refers to the object of the sentence, *that or which* can be omitted.

Examples:
The storybooks (that / which) *I enjoyed most when I was young were* The Moomins *by Tove Jansson.*

Academic writing: A review

1 **Match the words with the extracts from a film review.**

> acting   cinematography   costume design   plot   screenplay   setting   soundtrack

a Fast-paced and full of twists and turns. It was never boring.

....

b The story takes place in the 1950s in a seaside town in Italy.

....

c Beautifully shot on location along the coast near Naples.

....

d Excellent performances from all the cast, especially the main characters.

....

e The dialogue cleverly reveals the secret motivations of the characters.

....

f The music subtly reflects the inner tensions of the characters' inner emotions.

....

g Fantastic recreation of the beautifully elegant fashions of the period.

....

2 **Read the book review on the next page. Which of these are mentioned in the review?**

Author ☐	Recommendation ☐	Type of book ☐
Overall opinion ☐	Style ☐	A weakness or flaw ☐
Plot summary ☐	Title ☐	Unique features ☐

War of the Worlds is a sci-fi novel written by H. G. Wells which was first published in 1898. It is one of the earliest books to describe the invasion of Earth by an alien species and is a classic of sci-fi literature. Narrated in the first person as an eyewitness account, it describes how Martians invade Earth and immediately engage in massive destruction of the cities and populations. The main focus of the plot is not on the characters but on the sequence of horrifying events as humans realise they are no longer in control. What is so remarkable about this novel, however, is that it was written well before the days of space travel and describes technology that was not invented until many years later. The story is gripping and also disturbing because it is described in such realistic detail. I recommend it to any fans of sci-fi and adventure fiction.

3   **Read the task. Use the graphic organiser to make notes. Then write a review of 140–190 words in your notebook.**

Think of a book or film that you enjoyed. Tell us your opinion of it and why you enjoyed it. Was there anything you disliked about it? Tell us who you would recommend this book or film to.

WRITING TIP

When writing a review, it is a good idea to give concrete reasons for your opinions. Instead of saying, 'It had a good story,' you can say 'The story was interesting because there were so many unexpected twists.'

Book review

	Title and author / director
	Type of book / film

Main characters and plot summary

....

Unique features

....

	How did it make you feel?
	What did you dislike?
	Overall opinion
	Who would enjoy this book?

Check your progress

Vocabulary

1 **Complete the descriptions with words from the box.**

> apocalyptic   comforting   costume
> dystopian   escapism   realistic
> scenario   set   sinister   visual

A   There are many sci-fi films that depict a post-…… ………………[1] future set in the aftermath of some kind of disaster. This ………………[2] view of the future usually centres on a ………………[3] where a few humans have managed to survive and are trying to salvage some remnants of the world they have lost. Often, such disasters bring out the more ………………[4] side of human nature as people compete with each other for dwindling resources. The result is a disturbingly ………………[5] view of the future.

B   In contrast, there have been a number of TV series that portray a romantic and ………………[6] view of the past. Known as historical or ………………[7] dramas, they are often

………………[8] in a time before our lives were dominated by technology and provide a welcome feeling of ………………[9]. Part of their popularity also stems from the ………………[10] appeal of elegant fashions, vintage cars and a more luxurious lifestyle which some people complain is not realistic at all.

Which of these would you prefer to watch and why?

…………………………………………………………

Grammar

2 **Circle the correct word(s) to complete each sentence.**

a   The film had a very high budget, but the critics' response was *disappointed / disappointing*.

b   The *excited / exciting* fans waited for hours outside the theatre to see their favourite actors.

c   The audience were so *shocking / shocked* by the final scene that they walked out.

d   *What makes / What makes it* this exhibition stand out is the perfect use of colour and light.

e   The best things about the musical *were / they were* the wonderful costumes and set design.

f   It is the excellent performances by the two lead actors *that / what* make this play so compelling.

Reading

3   Read the article and think of an appropriate title for it.

....

There are so many reasons to join our drama club! The main reason is that it's a lot of fun! Not only that, but you get to make friends and collaborate in a positive supportive environment. Although you may feel nervous at first, you'll soon gain confidence, which will benefit other aspects of your schoolwork, such as giving presentations and working on group projects. Finally, it's not just about drama, it's about expressing yourself and finding out what you are capable of and what you can become.

4   Answer the questions.

a   Who is the article for? ....

b   What is the purpose of the article?

....

....

c   What drawback does the article mention?

....

....

d   What other drawbacks can you think of?

....

....

Writing

5   Choose one of these questions and make notes of your ideas. Then write a response of about 150 words in your notebook.

Do TV costume dramas give us a realistic portrayal of history or are they just escapism?

Do dystopian dramas help to warn us about the dangers of nuclear disaster and climate breakdown, or do they give us a false sense of security?

REFLECTION

Write answers to these questions in your notebook.

a   Describe three ways that art and culture are important in your life.

b   What kind of art or culture would you like to be involved in?

c   Why is critical evaluation important when reading a text?

d   What criteria would you use to evaluate a film or a book as 'good' or 'bad'?

e   What are three important points to remember when writing a review?

9 Life choices

Think about it: Big decisions

1   **Read the quiz and answer the questions.**

What kind of decision-maker are you? Circle your answers.

Type 1:

1   I find it helps to write a list of pros and cons before I decide anything.
True   False

2   I like to consult friends or family before making a decision.
True   False

3   I generally consider all aspects of a problem before reaching a solution.
True   False

4   I always look up reviews before deciding what to buy.
True   False

5   I tend to make a plan and then stick to it no matter what happens.
True   False

Type 2:

1   When I find something I like, I usually like it immediately or not at all.
True   False

2   I often buy things on impulse.
True   False

3   Sometimes I decide on something and change my mind at the last minute.
True   False

4   I often make a decision quickly but then immediately regret it.
True   False

5   I generally voice my opinions immediately without thinking too much.
True   False

Your score: Type 1 ....   Type 2 ....

If type 1 describes you, you are a systematic type of decision-maker. You gather information carefully before making a decision. You are cautious. You prefer to take time and think through all sides of the problem. You plan your goals and work towards them carefully and rationally.

....

If type 2 describes you, you are a spontaneous type of decision-maker. You tend to make decisions quickly based on your feelings or instincts. You are often impulsive and willing to take risks. You are flexible and don't mind adjusting your plans if the situation changes.

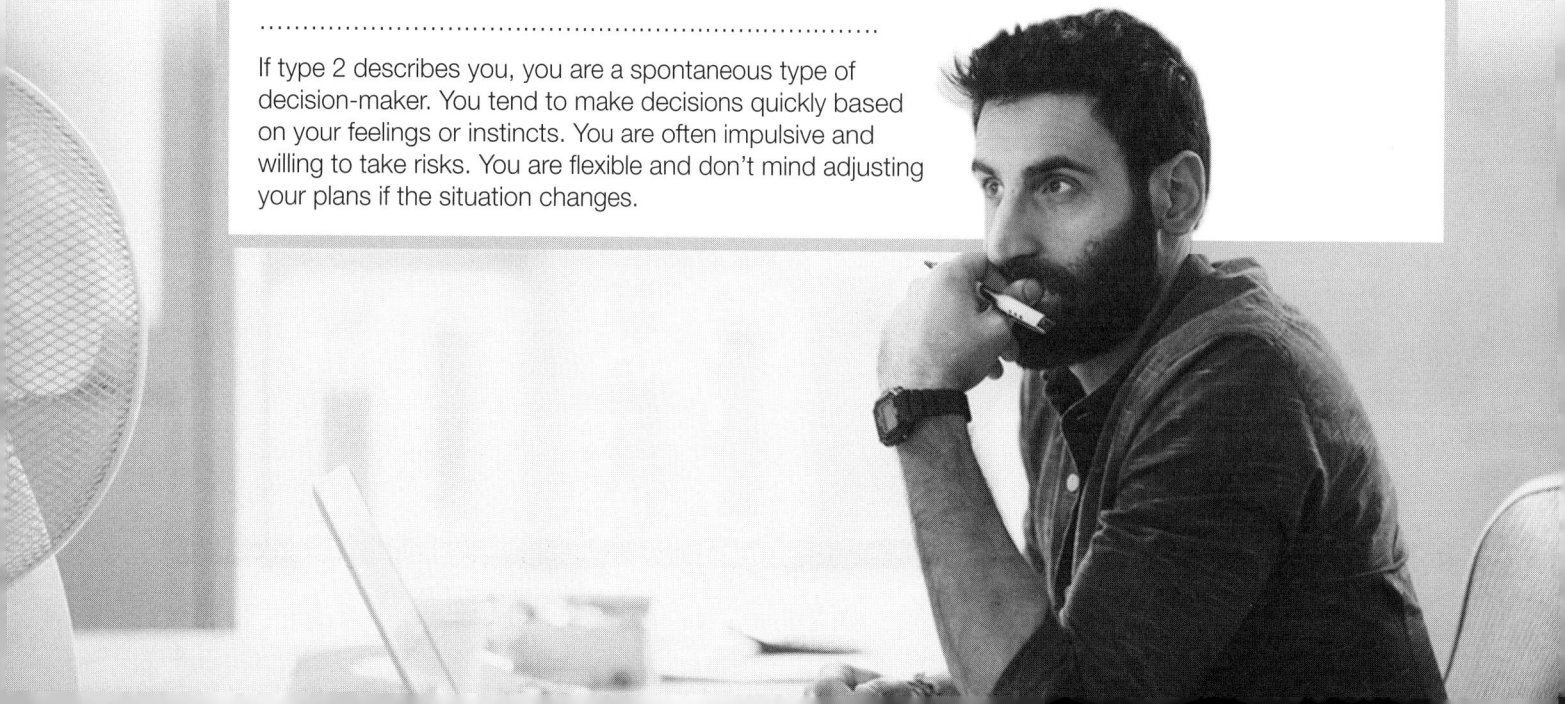

2   Read the problems and give each person some advice.

a   **Daniel:** I want to give up eating meat because I think it's good for the planet. Raising animals for food is really bad to the environment and I think we should all make an effort, however small, to reduce it. But sausages are my favourite food and I'm worried I won't be able to stay meat-free! How can I make sure I don't give up?

Your advice: ....

b   **Nadine:** I promised my best friend that I would go to a concert with her next weekend. But now I've found out that there's a family dinner the same day and my uncles and cousins are all coming over, so I have to be there. I wish I hadn't promised to go to the concert but don't want to let my friend down. What shall I do?

Your advice: ....

c   **Ramesh:** I need to decide what to study at college next year. My parents want me to choose something safe like accounting or law, where a job with a good salary is more or less guaranteed. Of course, I respect my parents' opinions and want them to be proud of me. But I'm more interested in art and drama. How can I explain it to them?

Your advice: ....

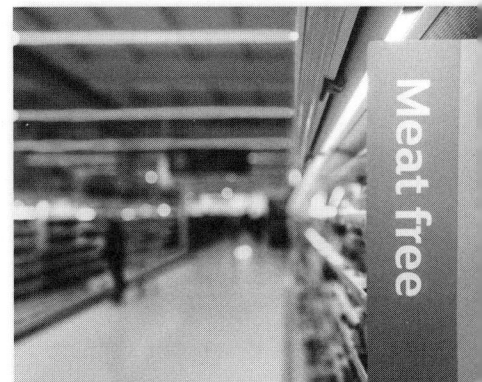

3   Answer these questions about the people in Exercise 2.

a   Who faces a dilemma between two good choices? ....

b   Who has to decide between a conventional and a more controversial choice?

....

c   Who wants to make a personal decision based on its global impact?

....

d   Who wants validation from their family? ....

e   Who regrets something they have done? ....

f   Who is worried about the strength of their willpower? ....

g   Who is facing a life decision? ....

Challenge
4   Write a brief description of a dilemma or difficult choice you have faced in the past. How did you solve it? Write a paragraph in your notebook.

Technology and environmental science: Homes for a better planet

1   **Read the title of the article and look at the photo. What do you think the article is about?**

....

Going zero waste

Plastic is everywhere in our world and has hundreds of different uses that range from food storage to healthcare, but do you know how plastic is made? Some types of plastic are bio-based and made from raw materials such as cornflour, vegetable fats and bacteria. Other kinds of plastic are **synthetic**. They are made from fossil fuels, usually crude oil or natural gas.

Plastic affects the environment in a number of different ways. First, it uses raw materials, in particular oil and gas, that are non-renewable. Second, the process of producing plastic requires intense heat, which uses a lot of energy. The most significant impact is that plastic – even the bio-based kind – can **persist** for centuries. Not only that, but when oil-based plastics eventually break down, they release greenhouse gases and **leak** chemicals into the soil. Another negative effect is that microplastics find their way into the oceans and rivers where they endanger birds, fish and wildlife that mistake them for food. They could be harming humans as well because they are present in seafood and drinking water that we consume.

So what can we do as individuals that will have an impact on the mountain of plastic that goes into our landfills every day? One thing we can do is to change our shopping habits. Here are some suggestions for small changes that will help to make your life zero waste and can help to reduce plastic, just one step at a time.

- Always take a reusable bag with you when you go shopping.
- Take washable reusable produce bags for fruit and vegetables.
- Use a reusable water bottle or beverage cup (made from glass, metal, ceramic or bamboo).
- Choose food products that come in cardboard or paper packaging.

HOW LONG UNTIL IT'S DECOMPOSED?
ESTIMATED DECOMPOSITION RATES OF WASTE IN OUR OCEANS

REDUC
REUSE
RECYCL

BANANA PEEL
3-4 weeks

PAPER BAG
1 month

APPLE C
2 mont

WOOL SOCK
1-5 years

MILK CARTON
5 years

PLASTIC BAG
10-20 years

LEATHER SI
25-40 yea

FOAMED PLASTIC CUP
50 years

NYLON FABRI
30-40 years

RUBBER BOOT SOLE
50-80 years

BATTERY
100 years

ALUMINUM CAN
200-500 years

PLASTIC BOTTLE
450 years

DISPOSABLE DIAPER
450-550 years

MONOFILAMENT
FISHING LINE
600 years

GLASS BOTTLE
1 million years

- Avoid individually packaged food like teabags and buy loose tea instead.
- Choose shampoo, soap and laundry soap that comes in bars and needs no packaging.
- Go to grocery shops that refill your containers of flour, sugar, oil and other products.
- Instead of buying ketchup or yogurt in plastic cartons, make your own!

These are just some ideas for starting to go zero waste. If you want to learn more, join our zero-waste challenge and take part in our nationwide week of activities for plastic-free living!

> **synthetic:** made from artificial substances
>
> **persist:** endure, not decay
>
> **leak:** escape, spill

2 **Complete these sentences with information from the article.**
   Use one word in each gap.

   a There are two types of plastic: .... and synthetic.

   b The production of plastic uses .... and raw materials.

   c Plastics harm our environment because they don't ....

   ....

   d Birds, fish and humans are in danger of .... plastic.

   e Cutting down on plastic will help protect the environment and reduce

   ....

3 **Find these words in the article and write a definition for each one.**
   Then check your definitions in a dictionary.

   a non-renewable ....

   b microplastics ....

   c zero waste ....

4 **Which of the suggestions in this article have you tried?**
   Which ones would you like to try?
   Add three more ideas to the list.

   ....

   ....

   ....

   ....

   ....

   ....

Challenge

5 **Keep a diary for three days, listing all the plastic that you use or buy.**
   Then think of ways to avoid using them.

Use of English: Future forms

USE OF ENGLISH

> **To:** [   ]
>
> Hi Sushila!
>
> How's it going with your university applications? I'm taking my entrance exams next week and I'm really nervous! I'm sure I'll pass, but my grades may not be good enough to get the place I want. I could end up having to do my exams all over again! I can't wait for the holidays. This time next month we'll have finished all our exams and we'll be swimming and surfing at the seaside. We're going to have an amazing time!
>
> See you soon, Emilia

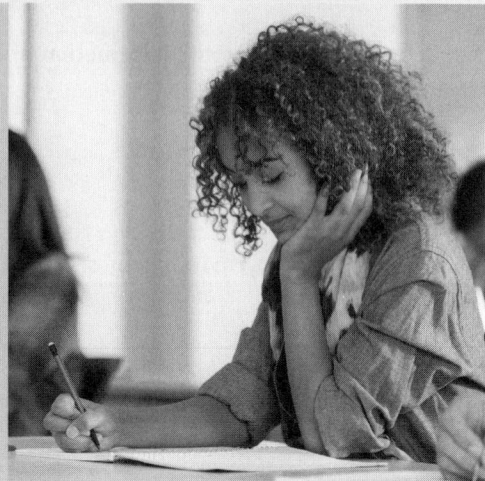

Check!

1   Read the conversation above. Underline the verbs with future forms.

Notice

2   Match the verb forms from the conversation with these meanings.

   a   an action or event that is in progress in the future ....

   b   a future intention ....

   c   talk about a future event as if seen in the past ....

   d   talk about future possibility ....

   e   make predictions we are certain about ....

   f   talk about future events we are less certain about ....

   g   talk about future arrangements ....

Focus

3   Complete the sentences with words from the box.

am going   be doing   could   may   starting   will have

   a   I am not sure yet, but I ....take a year off before going to uni.

b I've been offered a job at the newspaper and I'm .... on Monday.

c In five years' time, we ....forgotten all about exams!

d What will you .... ten years from now?

e You .... study arts or science – you're equally good in both.

f I .... to study photography and nothing will stop me!

Practice

4 **Circle the correct word to complete each sentence.**
Identify the meaning in each one by writing F (future possibility), P (permission) or A (ability).

a You *can / could* receive an answer later this week.   ....

b You *can / could* switch on your phones when the exam is over.   ....

c We should leave now, or we *can / could* miss the train.   ....

d You'd better take an umbrella because it *could / can* rain later.   ....

e Our expert counsellors *can / could* help you with your application.   ....

> **GET IT RIGHT!**
>
> *Could* is used for future possibility.
> *Can* is used for ability or permission.
>
> **Examples:**
> You **could** think about applying for college next year. (future possibility)
>
> You **can** send in your applications by email. (ability/permission)

5 **Improve these sentences by using a more suitable future form.**

a What do you do after school today?

....

b We have a party on Saturday.

....

c It isn't definite yet, but we will move to another town.

....

d By this time next month, I will live here for five years.

....

Challenge

6 **Answer these questions using future forms. Write the answers in your notebook.**

a What is one thing you are sure you will do next year?

b What is one thing you could possibly do next year?

c What is one thing you will have done by next year?

Use of English: *-ing* clauses

USE OF ENGLISH

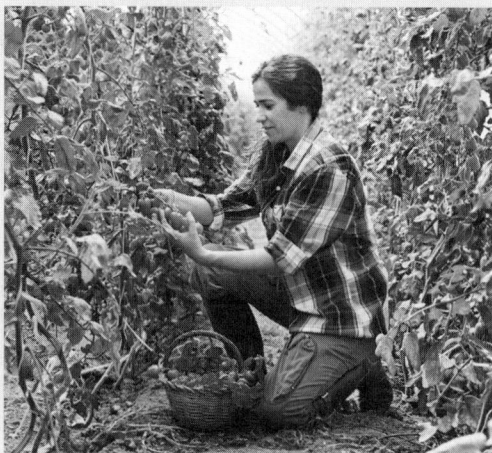

Working on a farm last summer, I realised how much I loved growing fruit and vegetables.

A Having always enjoyed singing at school, I auditioned for a TV musical talent show.

B Looking at my phone for the hundredth time, I decided it was time to take a break from social media.

C Never having learned how to cook, I decided to take a cookery class.

D Having said goodbye to my family, I set off to travel around the world for a year.

E Waiting for the bus, I noticed an advert for volunteers at the local community kitchen.

F After finishing my art degree, I selected a course in graphic design.

G Not knowing anyone in my new neighbourhood, I joined a local cycling club.

Check!

1   Read the sentences above about people who made life decisions. Which sentences use an *-ing* clause for the following?

   a   to give a reason for an action   ....

   b   to describe two things happening at the same time   ....

   c   to describe a sequence of events   ....

   d   use an *-ing* form after a preposition   ....

Notice

2   Answer these questions about the sentences.

   a   Which sentences use the past perfect participle?   ....

   b   Which sentences use a negative form?   ....

Focus

3   **Rewrite the underlined part of each sentence using an *-ing* clause.**

   a   .... <u>After I talked</u> with a careers advisor, I started looking for a course in nursing.

   b   .... <u>She saw</u> lots of plastic being thrown away, (so) she decided to stop using plastic bags.

   c   .... <u>While we lived</u> in France, we learned a lot about French history and culture.

d .... <u>He drank</u> a coffee (and) he watched the news on TV.

e .... <u>I always had</u> a part-time job, (so) I had plenty of work experience.

Practice

4   **Correct the following sentences so that the subjects of both clauses are the same.**

a   Cooking breakfast for his family, the smoke alarm suddenly went off.

....

b   Not knowing how to get to her house, their GPS gave them directions.

....

c   Arriving ten minutes late, the lesson had already started.

....

d   Leaving her home without an umbrella, it started to rain.

....

Challenge

5   **Rewrite each sentence using words from the box and an *-ing* form.**

Despite   After   Before   In spite of   Instead of   While

a   Although they had arrived early, they saw that the train station was very crowded.

Despite having arrived early, they saw that the train station was very crowded.

b   First, she did some research. Then she wrote to several companies for information.

....

c   He worked full-time in a bank and at the same time he studied part-time at college.

....

d   She had never been to China but she spoke Chinese fluently.

....

e   He only looked for a new job when he left his old job.

....

f   They wanted to visit New Zealand but eventually decided to go somewhere nearer.

....

> **GET IT RIGHT!**
>
> Remember that the subject of the *-ing* clause and the main clause should be the same.
>
> **Examples:**
> *Having coffee with a friend, my phone wasn't working.* (incorrect)
>
> *Having coffee with a friend, I noticed that my phone wasn't working.* (correct)

Academic writing: An article

1 What is a gap year? What are three questions you have about taking a gap year?

....

....

....

2 Read the article. Does it answer your questions from Exercise 1?

Making the most of your gap year!

So you're in your last year of school, you've sent in your university applications and you're about to finish your exams. How do you feel? Are you ready to go straight into a new academic environment, with all the stress of essays, assignments and deadlines? Or do you think it might be a good time to take a break? For me, the answer was clear.

A lot of people – especially parents – worry that taking a gap year will set you back academically and that you won't feel like settling down to study at the end of your gap year. In my case, it was just the opposite. At the end of my gap year, I was sure about what I wanted to study and felt even more focused on my goals. Studies have shown that students who take a gap year end up with better academic results and are more involved in campus activities than those who go straight to university.

Another reason people hesitate is that they think a year off won't look good on their curriculum vitae. I think that depends on how you plan your gap year. It's not always about travelling! It can be anything you want, like learning a language or working as an intern or a volunteer, all of which can help you gain skills that will look really good on your CV. In fact, many universities look favourably on students who have worked or volunteered for a year before starting university.

Having finished my first year at uni, it is only now that I realise how much I learned during my gap year. I had time to reflect on what I want to do in life and what kind of person I want to be. I learned to manage my time – as well as my finances! – independently. I made new friends and learned new skills that have helped me feel more confident. Taking a gap year was definitely the right choice for me.

> **WRITING TIP**
>
> When writing an article, think about the topic from your readers' point of view. What do you think they will be most interested in? What will they find most useful?

3 Answer these questions about the article.

a What is the purpose of the article?

....

b Who is the intended audience? ....

c   Does the writer give a balanced view of the pros and cons of taking a gap

year? ....

d   What benefits of taking a gap year does the writer mention?

....

e   What negatives of <u>not</u> taking a gap year are implied?

....

f   What kind of information does the writer include in the conclusion?
How effective is this at persuading the reader?

....

4   **Study the article again. Find examples of the following and underline them.**
Think about how they are used to make the article more persuasive.

informal language   humour   asking questions
giving a hint   an *-ing* clause

5   **Read the task. Use the graphic organiser to make notes.**
Then write the article in your notebook in 300–350 words.

You are about to finish university and you have just been offered two work
opportunities. One is an office job that may lead to a permanent well-paid
position as a manager. The other is to work as volunteer on a wildlife reserve for
six months with all expenses paid. Write an article about your decision and what
effect it had on you.

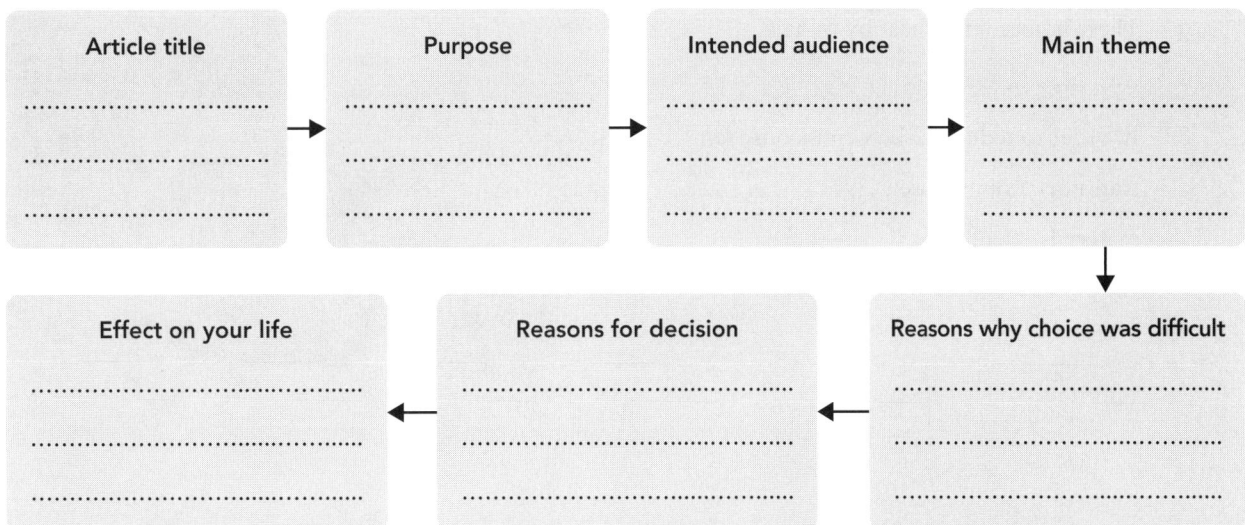

Article title	Purpose	Intended audience	Main theme
....	....	....	....
....	....	....	....
....	....	....	....

Effect on your life	Reasons for decision	Reasons why choice was difficult
....	....	....
....	....	....
....	....	....

Check your progress

Vocabulary

1 **Complete the sentences with words from the box.**

> biodegradable   controversial   dilemma
> locally sourced   radical   raw material
> thermal barrier   willpower

a Have you ever faced a .... that was difficult for you to solve?

b You must have needed .... to give up using social media.

c The use of nuclear plants to produce energy is a .... issue.

d Making 3D printed houses seemed like a .... idea a few years ago.

e Plastic harms the environment because it isn't ....

f The .... for plastic is usually crude oil or gas.

g These homes retain heat by using a ....

h In order to reduce carbon emissions from transportation, we use .... materials.

Grammar

2 **Circle the correct word(s) to complete each sentence.**

a We *may* / *will* go to live in New York next year, but we aren't sure.

b I've decided that from now on I won't *be eating* / *have eaten* meat any more.

c I can't see you tomorrow because I'll *work* / *be working*.

d *Having saved* / *Saving* up some money, I started to plan my trip.

e *Having worked* / *Working* at the urban farm, I met lots of people who care about the environment.

f Instead of *use* / *using* fossil fuels, we try to use renewables.

Reading

3 **Read the article and answer the questions that follow.**

No New Clothes!

Hi everyone! I've finally decided to take up the No New Clothes Challenge! What does it mean? It means that I promise not to buy any new clothes for a whole year. Sounds crazy, right? You all know how much I love shopping for clothes. It's almost a kind of therapy for me. I often buy new clothes when I don't even need them. But recently I watched a documentary about the environmental impact of fast fashion. How we're convinced that we constantly need new clothing that gets worn once or twice and then just ends up in a landfill as soon as the fashions change. So I decided to change my consumerist mindset and just make do with the clothing that I already have. If I really need something different, I can go to a charity shop or visit a vintage and second-hand clothing website. So far, it's been almost a month and I've been amazed by my willpower! But it's not just about the environment – who knew that No New Clothes would save me time and money as well!

a Who do you think is the intended audience for this article?

....

b What is the purpose of the article?

....

c What reasons does the article mention for not buying any new clothes?

....

....

d What reason does the writer suggest for why people buy new clothes so frequently?

....

e What does the writer mean by a 'consumerist mindset'?

....

....

f What other advantages of not buying new clothes can you think of?

....

....

Writing

4 **Read the question and make notes of your ideas. Then write a response of about 150 words in your notebook.**

You have made a decision to reduce your environmental impact by not using any plastic bottles or plastic bags. Explain the reasons that led to your decision and how you went about making this lifestyle change. What effect did it have on your life?

REFLECTION

Write answers to these questions in your notebook.

a What do you think will be an important life decision you will have to make in the future?

b What did you learn about how our lifestyles can be more sustainable?

c Has your attitude to making consumer choices changed after studying this unit?

d What is one lifestyle change that you think everyone will have to make in the future?

e What are three pieces of advice you would give to someone writing an article?

10 Voyage to success

Think about it: Determined or just plain stubborn?

1   Read these situations and match them with the descriptions.

Felix wanted to study drama and applied to a drama school, but didn't get a place right away, so he decided to try something easier instead.

Josh wanted to go on a mountain climbing trip, but his parents thought it was too dangerous, so he agreed to go hiking instead.

Sabina was nervous about taking part in the school play, but she practised techniques for staying calm and in the end she was a huge success.

The weather forecast predicted rain and thunderstorms, but **Tina** insisted on having her birthday party in the garden. It poured with rain and everyone got soaked.

Sanjay explained to his grandparents that everyone uses online banking these days, but they preferred to keep paying their bills by cheque.

When **Victor** asked for a 5% pay rise, his manager asked him to consider 2% and suggested he could work at home two days a week.

Anya's parents wanted to move to a house in the country, but before deciding, they had a meeting with all the members of their family and listened carefully to their opinions.

Hugo failed his driving test four times, but he didn't give up and finally passed on the fifth try.

Who...

a   overcame an obstacle?   ....

b   showed determination?   ....

c   gave up easily?   ....

d   agreed on a compromise?   ....

e   was rather stubborn?   ....

f   tried to negotiate?   ....

g   resisted change?   ....

h   was very open-minded?   ....

2   **Complete the sentences with words from the box.**
   Which statements are true about you?

> a solution   doubts   personality   pressure   plans   succeed

a   Some people think I have a **stubborn** ....

b   I'm good at **negotiating** .... to a disagreement.

c   It's difficult for me to **resist** the .... to conform to social norms.

d   I don't usually **give up** my .... without a struggle.

e   I am **determined** to .... in my future career.

f   I am good at **overcoming** my ....

3   **Read the description in the speech bubble and underline features**
   of connected speech. Then read the text aloud.

a   Find four examples of consonant to vowel linking.

   ....

   ....

b   Find five examples of vowel to vowel linking.
   Write /r/, /w/, or /j/.

   ....

c   Find three examples of sound twinning.

   ....

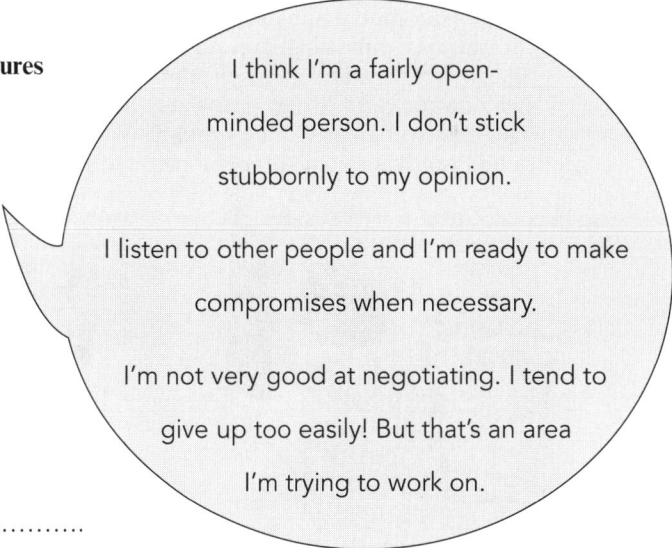

I think I'm a fairly open-minded person. I don't stick stubbornly to my opinion.

I listen to other people and I'm ready to make compromises when necessary.

I'm not very good at negotiating. I tend to give up too easily! But that's an area I'm trying to work on.

Challenge

4   **Write three sentences about your personality in your notebook.**
   Use the words in bold in Exercise 2.

Sociology: Creative problem-solving

1   **Think about a problem you faced recently.
    How did you go about solving it? List three steps in your notebook.**

2   **Read the article and complete the flowchart.**

Creative problem-solving

Creative problem-solving is a way of coming up with new and original solutions to a problem. Using a structured process to come up with new ideas is a way to **harness** the creativity of your team and develop a creative problem-solving **mindset**.

Let's assume that you have identified a problem in your workplace. For example, you have found that workers in your office prefer to use single-use plastic coffee cups instead of bringing their own reusable mugs. You think this is a problem because it creates too much plastic waste.

You can use a tool known as 'starbursting' to think about this problem as a series of *wh-* questions. Write your problem in the middle of the board and draw a six-pointed star around it. Each point of the star will represent a question starting with *who*, *what*, *when*, *where*, *why* and *how*. These questions can help you to look at the problem from different angles and define the problem more accurately.

Gathering data about the issue, for example by carefully observing behaviour, will also help to define the problem.

The next step is to generate ideas for solving the problem. A technique known as 'brainstorming' involves discussing ideas in a group. Participants come up with as many ideas as they can – no matter how unrealistic or unlikely – and use this to generate further ideas from the group. This type of divergent thinking involves spreading a wide net to capture as many ideas as you can without judging them.

After generating ideas, it is time to evaluate them. This part of the process involves narrowing down your list of ideas to a shortlist of those that are most likely to be effective. This is known as convergent thinking. Once you have arrived at your final decision, you and your team can start planning how to **implement** the decision and what kind of resources you will need to put your plan into action.

harness: make use of	**implement:** make something happen
mindset: way of thinking	

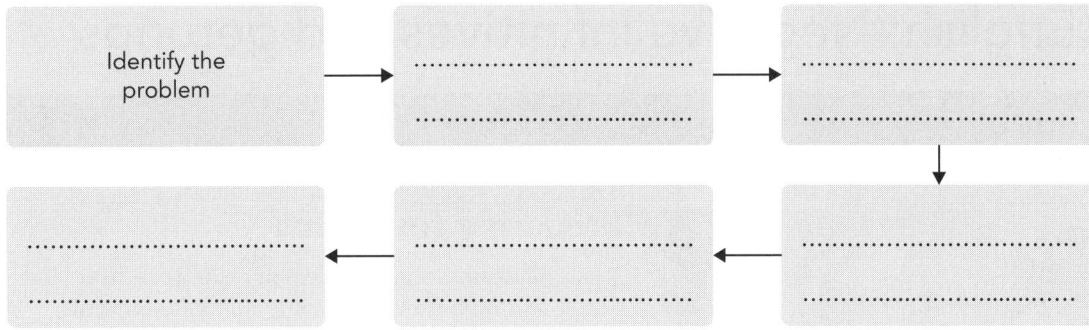

Identify the
problem

3   **Answer these questions.**

   a   Who is this article for? ....

   b   What is the difference between divergent and convergent thinking?

   ....

   c   What are starbursting and brainstorming examples of?

   ....

4   **Using the plastic cups example mentioned in the article, write ideas for the following in your notebook.**

   a   five wh- questions to ask about the problem

   b   five ways to observe behaviour related to use of plastic cups

   c   five ideas for reducing use of plastic cups and promoting reusable cups

   d   three reasons why your choice of solution would be effective

Challenge

5   **Think of a problem in your school or classroom. Follow the steps in the creative thinking process to come to a solution. Write the problem and the solution here.**

   Problem: ....

   ....

   Solution: ....

   ....

Use of English: Negative infinitives and gerunds

USE OF ENGLISH

Preparing for exams

It's difficult not to get stressed at exam time. But studying long hours and staying up late the night before an exam isn't always a good idea! Not getting enough sleep can affect your concentration. And studies have shown that not taking breaks can also cause your attention span to decrease. In order not to get burned out, plan to take short breaks at regular intervals. And don't use them to check your phone! Do some gentle stretching exercises, get a drink of water (not drinking enough water can also affect your memory) or make a healthy snack instead.

Check!

1   Read the information above. Underline the negative infinitive and gerund forms.

Notice

2   What do you notice about the position of the word 'not' in negative infinitives?

    ....

Focus

3   **Complete these sentences using negative infinitive or gerund forms.**

   a   Eat a healthy breakfast the day of the exam.

       .... breakfast will affect your energy levels later.

   b   Make a plan for how much time to spend on each subject.

       .... can mean you will not be able to cover everything.

   c   Take regular breaks so that you don't feel stressed.

       In order .... you should take regular breaks.

   d   If you are struggling with a problem, ask for help.

       It's important .... with problems alone.

   e   Avoid stress by packing your schoolbag the night before.

       .... your bag could cause you extra stress in the morning.

Practice

4   Complete each sentence using the negative infinitive form of a word from the box.

be   eat   get   panic   study

a   It's a good idea .... sugary food for breakfast.

b   Try .... late on the day of the exam.

c   It's better .... long periods without a break.

d   It's sometimes difficult .... when you see the exam paper.

e   Make sure .... dehydrated by drinking plenty of water.

5   Circle the best option to complete each sentence.
Both options are grammatically correct, but which is more likely?

a   They *didn't agree / agreed not* to make any noise in the library.

b   In order to avoid *feeling / not feeling* stressed, plan your revision time carefully.

c   We *weren't allowed / were allowed not* to speak during the exam.

d   Students *aren't encouraged / are encouraged not* to leave any questions unanswered.

e   They stopped us from *using / not using* our phones in the exam.

Challenge

6   Write four pieces of advice for someone preparing for exams.
Use negative infinitives or gerunds.

a   .... might make you late for your exam.

b   .... could make you tired and lose energy.

c   If you want to reduce distractions, it's better

....

d   To stay healthy and calm, it's a good

idea ....

Use of English: Past modals

USE OF ENGLISH

Leon: Can you tell us how you got started in your career as an artist? It can't have been easy.

Sofia: No, it wasn't. You see, I had a well-paid job in a PR company, and I could have worked there all my life and would probably have been promoted to managing director eventually. But I decided it wasn't for me!

Leon: So you took a risk, even though keeping your job might have worked out better for you financially? You must have been quite worried about whether you would succeed or not.

Sofia: Yes, I was. But luckily, I got a grant from an arts foundation that lasted a whole year. Without it, I wouldn't have been able to manage. Looking back, I probably should have taken the plunge a lot earlier!

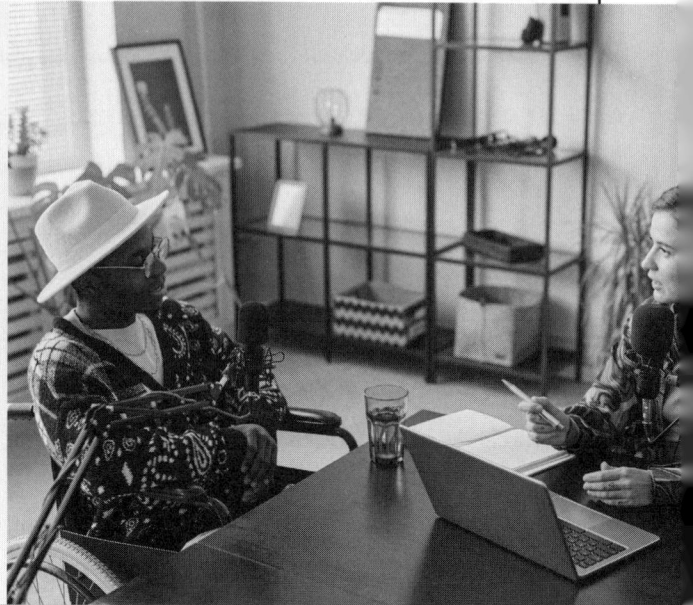

Check!

1 Read the conversation above and underline examples of past modals.

2 Which modal expresses the following?

a something that was very likely ....

b something that was almost certainly true ....

c something that was possible ....

d something that didn't happen ....

e something that happened ....

3 Circle the correct answer.

Past modals are used to refer to past situations that are *real / imaginary*.

Notice

4 Answer these questions about the passive.

a Which modal in the conversation uses the passive form? ....

b How is the passive formed? ....

Focus

5 **Rewrite the underlined part of each sentence using a past modal.**

a ....<u>I am sure she was</u> nervous about performing in the concert.

b .... <u>It is possible that he found</u> a better job somewhere else.

c .... <u>I am sure that he didn't know</u> about the meeting.

d .... I <u>regretted not learning</u> another language when I was younger.

e .... <u>I was able to pass the exam with</u> the help of my teacher.

Practice

6 **Correct the mistakes.**

a The meeting was really important. They could invite you.

....

b If we had logged on to the website earlier, the tickets wouldn't be sold out.

....

c You didn't speak with a counsellor. That was a mistake.

....

d Oh no! I left my phone on the bus. But that's impossible!

....

> **GET IT RIGHT!**
>
> Remember to use *have* + past participle after the modal when referring to imaginary past events.
>
> **Example:**
> *If I hadn't had my phone, I would get lost.* (incorrect)
>
> *If I hadn't had my phone, I would have got lost.* (correct)

Challenge

7 **Read these situations. Then write three sentences about each one using past modals.**

a Cesar wanted to join the football team, but he was worried that he wouldn't have enough time to study.

....

....

b Nadine went to the airport to catch a plane to Italy, but she left her passport at home and she missed the plane.

....

....

c Marta and Luis went to the theatre to see a concert, but the building was empty and all the lights were off.

....

....

Academic writing: Opinion essay – review

1　**What is your opinion about written exams?**
Complete the sentences using your own ideas.

　　a　Written exams are useful because

　　　　...

　　b　To do well in written exams, you need skills such as

　　　　...

　　c　There are alternative types of assessment, such as coursework, which

　　　　...

2　**Read the essay question. Then read the list of advantages and disadvantages.**
Which of the points are in favour of the statement and which are against?
Write F or A.

It is generally accepted that traditional written exams are the fairest way of
measuring students' intelligence. However, this type of assessment does not always
give an accurate picture of their abilities. To what extent do you agree?

		WRITING TIP
a Create competition and motivation	....	When writing an opinion essay, think carefully about the opposing point of view and explain why you don't think those arguments are valid.
b Cause stress and anxiety	....	
c Test ability to pass exams	....	
d Don't test skills such as creativity	....	
e Failure causes damage to self-esteem	....	
f Easier to evaluate and compare results	....	
g Test ability to express ideas in writing	....	
h Students can memorise their answers	....	
i Evaluation is not always objective	....	
j Fewer opportunities to cheat	....	

　　　　...

　　　　...

3　**Add two more points to the list in Exercise 2, either for or against.**

4   Select your main arguments from Exercise 3 and write them in the organiser.
Then write some key words and phrases for your introduction and conclusion.

Introduction with main idea

....

....

....

Main reason for or against

....

Supporting arguments

1 ....

2 ....

3 ....

Conclusion with your opinion

....

....

....

5   Write the essay in your notebook. Aim for 250–300 words.

Check your progress

Vocabulary

1 Complete the text with words from the box.

```
compromise    determination    give up
negotiate    open-minded    overcome
resist    stubbornness
```

The path to success

Is ....¹ the key to success?

It's not ....² if you just want

to stick to your goals and do your best to

........................³ obstacles to achieve them.

It's sometimes hard to ....⁴ the

temptation to ....⁵ and accept a

........................⁶. Although it's important to

be ....⁷ towards other people's

opinions, you should learn to ....⁸

with people calmly and confidently, so that you end

up with the result you really want.

Grammar

2 Correct the mistakes in each sentence.

a It's a good idea not use your phone before you go to sleep.

b In order not running out of energy, eat something healthy like a banana.

c I talked to the counsellor about not to take my exams until next year.

d He didn't answer my call. I think he should have turned off his phone.

e If I had known about the concert, I would book tickets earlier.

f You did really well on your test. You may have studied hard.

Reading

3 Read the article and answer the questions that follow.

Staying motivated is essential to achieving your goals. First, review your goals. Are they realistic within the timeframe you have planned? Try breaking them down into smaller steps so that you can monitor your progress more easily. Each time you achieve a goal, reward yourself with a small treat. What can you do if you lose motivation? Everyone can experience setbacks, but one way to tackle this is to find a friend and work together on helping each other to set and review your goals regularly. Another idea is to look for a video or book about someone who can inspire you. Or why not try taking a break to do something completely different? You'll come back feeling refreshed and reenergised.

a What do you think would be a good title for this article?

....

b Who do you think would find this article useful?

....

....

c What is the purpose of the article?

....

....

d When does the article advise you to take a break?

....

e What other ways of staying motivated can you think of?

....

....

....

Writing

4 Read the question and make a plan of your ideas. Then write an essay of around 300 words in your notebook.

It is often thought that encouraging competition to get the highest marks is a good way to motivate students to do their best. To what extent do you agree with this approach?

REFLECTION

Write answers to these questions in your notebook.

a What have you learned about determination in this unit?

b Give an example of a situation where you could use creative problem-solving.

c What personal qualities would you look for in someone that inspires you?

d Is there anything you wish you had done differently in the last school year?

e What advice would you give to yourself for the beginning of next year?

Key phrases bank

Unit 1

Reporting findings and drawing conclusions

What it shows is that…
… are thought to be…

Giving an opinion

It goes without saying that…
I would also add…
From my understanding…
As far as I'm concerned…
There's no doubt in my mind that…
I'd agree with that…
In my view…

Useful phrases for a discussion essay

On the one hand…
On the other hand…
It could be argued that…
This is evident in…

Unit 2

Discourse markers for attitude and sequencing

Firstly… Secondly…
First of all…
On top of that….
… and then…
In fact…
For a start…
What's more…
In the end…
I must admit…
To be honest…

Expressing cause and effect

… account for…
… because of…
… due to…

… give rise to…
… on account of…
… owing to…
… mean (that)…
As a consequence of…
As a result of…

Unit 3

Expressing certainty, possibility and uncertainty – informal

It's obvious…
I assume…
It's unclear…
Perhaps…
I'm sure…
There's a good chance…
I suppose…
It might…
I get the impression that…

Expressing certainty, possibility and uncertainty – formal

All the evidence supports the idea that…
There is a high possibility that…

Unit 4

Signposting

Let me start with…
Let's turn to…
Moving on to…
Let's look at…

Comparing and describing

… is less / greater / larger / smaller / fewer / more than…
… the most…
… the least…

Unit 5

Maintaining the interaction in a discussion

That's really interesting…
Why is that?
And what about you?
So what do you think…
And what about…

Impersonal language

This… is based on…
All those who were interviewed said that…
It is recommended that…
It would be advisable for…

Unit 6

Expressions to signpost important information

One of the main reasons…
The issue is not so much…

Asking for clarification

Could you explain…
When you talk about…
Are you suggesting that…
I guess what you're talking about…
I assume you don't mean…

Contrasting and disagreeing

Nevertheless…
It cannot be denied…
Even so…
However…
It is unreasonable…
Nonetheless…
… while…
The fact should not be ignored…

Unit 7

Talking about thinking

A theory has been put forward that…
… influence our thinking

Expressing manner and degree

… is approximately / roughly / particularly…
… altered dramatically

… exactly the opposite
… reasonably steady
… relatively stable
… increased dramatically
There has been a large fall / steady decline / significant increase
… has shown substantial growth / noteworthy improvement

Unit 8

Identifying non-essential information

… by the way…
… incidentally…

Summarising

In brief…
What I loved about… was
The one thing that…
The only thing is that…
The reason why…

Unit 9

Talking about the future

Tomorrow, I'm going to…
I don't know yet, but next weekend I might…
I have a plan for next weekend. I'm _____ing…
This time next year, I will be _____ing…
By this time next month, I will have…
During my lifetime, the world will…

Managing disagreement

While I understand your concerns about…, for me…
I agree that it's difficult to solve. What about if we…
Your point about… is valid. In my experience…
I understand your reasoning. My concerns are…
You've made some good points. It seems to me that…
I can see you've thought about it carefully. In my opinion…

Unit 10

Speculating

It seems to me that…
It appears as though…
It seems that…

Irregular verb table

Infinitive	Past simple	Past participle
be	was, were	been
begin	began	begun
break	broke	broken
bring	brought	brought
buy	bought	bought
build	built	built
choose	chose	chosen
come	came	come
cost	cost	cost
cut	cut	cut
do	did	done
draw	drew	drawn
drive	drove	driven
eat	ate	eaten
feel	felt	felt
find	found	found
fly	flew	flown
get	got	got
give	gave	given
go	went	gone
have	had	had
hold	held	held
hurt	hurt	hurt
keep	kept	kept
know	knew	known
leave	left	left
lead	led	led
let	let	let
lie	lay	lain
lose	lost	lost
make	made	made
mean	meant	meant
meet	met	met
pay	paid	paid
put	put	put
run	ran	run

Infinitive	Past simple	Past participle
say	said	said
see	saw	seen
sell	sold	sold
send	sent	sent
set	set	set
sit	sat	sat
speak	spoke	spoken
spend	spent	spent
stand	stood	stood
take	took	taken
teach	taught	taught
tell	told	told
think	thought	thought
understand	understood	understood
wear	wore	worn
win	won	won
write	wrote	written